A Sufi Perspective In Light of the Letter B

PROLOGUE TO DECODING
THE
QURAN

And

A Selection of Verses for Inquisitive and Free Minds

AHMED HULUSI

As with all my works, this book is not copyrighted.
As long as it remains faithful to the original,
it may be freely printed, reproduced, published and translated.
For the knowledge of ALLAH, there is no recompense.

A Sufi Perspective In Light of the Letter B

PROLOGUE TO DECODING THE QURAN

And

A Selection of Verses for Inquisitive and Free Minds

AHMED HULUSI

www.ahmedhulusi.org/en/

Translated by ALIYA ATALAY

ABOUT THE COVER

The black background of the front cover represents darkness and ignorance, while the white color of the letters represents light and knowledge.

The image is a Kufi calligraphy of the Word of Unity: *"La ilaha illallah; Muhammad Rasulullah"* which means,

"There is no concept such as 'god', there is only that which is denoted by the name Allah, and **Muhammad (SAW)** is the *Rasul* of this understanding."

The placement of the calligraphy, being on top and above everything else on the page, is a symbolic representation of the predominant importance this understanding holds in the author's life.

The green light, reflecting from the window of the Word of Unity, opens up from the darkness into luminosity to illustrate the light of Allah's *Rasul*. This light is embodied in the book's title through the author's pen and concretized as the color white, to depict the enlightenment the author aims to attain in this field. As the knowledge of Allah's *Rasul* disseminates, those who are able to evaluate this knowledge attain enlightenment, which is represented by the white background of the back cover.

Preface for Prologue to Decoding the Quran

"The part mirrors the whole" (Muhammad saw)

"All information is stored in every volume of space" (Quantum mechanics & the Holographic Principle)

He who wants to observe the reality can do so even on a single verse... Whether that be a manifestation in worldly form or a literal verse encrypted in the Quran... For just as the part contains the whole, a single verse can be a gateway into endless realizations, both inward and outward...

In this light, this tiny, yet very special selection and interpretation of verses by Ahmed Hulusi, released as a preliminary to *Decoding the Quran*, is like an invitation to man, to *read* and *know* himself... As only through a comprehensive knowledge of the self we have a real chance to know the One!

So let us forego our predetermined conditionings and *read* as though we are reading for the very first time...

Let us dive into this ocean of knowledge and melt away our constructs, fragmenting us from the Absolute One...

Let us enter this portal, stripped from the falsity of our identities, and begin the enthralling journey from ourselves, to ourselves!

"… from the One we came, and to the One we shall return…" (Quran 2:156)

Aliya Atalay
Istanbul, 2012

Translator's Note on The Beautiful Names

"Call upon Allah or call upon the *Rahman*, whichever you call upon, to HU belongs the Most Beautiful Names."[1]

"...In reality there is nothing in existence but His names"[2]

The Names of Allah, more commonly known as the Divine Names or the Most Beautiful Names, are the loci of manifestation. They are the attributes and relations through which Divine Self-disclosure occurs.

Everything derives its existence and originates from the meanings and structural qualities that are denoted by the Names of Allah; hence, the Names and their manifestations are our only means of knowing the reality of Allah.

Analogously, Muhammad (SAW) says "He who knows *himself* will know his *Rabb*[3]". Since the Divine Names comprise the essence of all things, and the essence of all things is ultimately One, he who knows his essential self will consequently know the One.

In this short book, Ahmed Hulusi takes us down a long corridor with 99 doors and presents a key for each of these doors that opens to our essential core realities. He asserts

---

[1] Quran 17:110
[2] Muhyiddin ibn al-Arabi, *Al-Futuhat Al-Makkiyya*, Chapter 177 (II 303.13)
[3] The reality of the Names comprising his essence.

that each individual manifestation, and hence each person, is composed of a unique configuration of Divine Names. Whether we call upon the door *Allah* or the door *Rahman*, whichever door we walk through, they all lead to *HU*! The only condition being, the abandoning of the constructed illusory self!

If you are willing to give up your limited self to the Unlimited Self and discover the infinite quantum potential within, walk with Ahmed Hulusi through this enchanting corridor and start knocking… for as Rumi says:

"Knock, and He'll open the door

Vanish, and He'll make you shine like the sun

Fall, and He'll raise you to the heavens

Become nothing, and He'll turn you into everything."

Aliya Atalay
Sydney, 2012

CONTENTS

1

INTRODUCTORY INFORMATION TO UNDERSTANDING THE QURAN

The original script of this work you've picked up to **READ** is not a book comprising *the orders and commands of a God up in the heavens, who apparently revealed it to his postman-prophet on earth*!

It is the **Knowledge of Reality** and the **System** (*Sunnatullah*)[4] *disclosed* by the *Rabb* of the worlds (the source of the infinite meanings of the Names), from the dimensional depths to the consciousness of **Rasulullah**[5], through the act of **revelation** (*irsal*)!

Let it be emphasized from the outset that...

This book is neither a translation nor an interpretation of the Quran. It can never replace the Quran! It is merely an attempt to share one or two aspects of the multi-layered meanings of the Quran!

This book is only a window looking at the Quran through the viewpoint endowed to Allah's servant, Ahmed Hulusi. Indeed, it is a reflection of only a part of the scene observed from this window!

---

[4] *Sunnatullah* denotes the laws and order of Allah, that is, the mechanics of the System and the laws that govern the manifested worlds.

[5] *Rasulullah* is the locus of Allah's knowledge, i.e. the focal point of the cosmos through which divine knowledge is expressed and disseminated.

The foundation of the viewpoint from this window is in accord with the following example:

When both eyes of a person are healthy and functional, the view is whole and clear. Those who don't have a full vision wear glasses or lenses. The **Quran** is like a lens bestowed by **Allah** so that one can obtain a clear and healthy vision of the two truths; the **Book of the Universe**, and the **System** (*Sunnatullah*), to **READ** them correctly.

In order to see the **Reality** as clear and one, we need the glasses of foresight (*basirah*) and knowledge, whereby the letter **B** comprises one lens, and the knowledge of the Absolute Self-sufficient One (*al-Ahad-us-Samad*) constitutes the other lens.

The former lens is the very first letter of the Quran; the letter **B**. Its meaning is revealed in Muhammad's (SAW) words "**The part is the same as the whole!**" which I have explained in consonance with the **Holographic Reality** in my book *The Observing One*. Every point perceived as a part or a unit in existence, contains the entire *al-Asma* (the Names) with their complete potentiality.

The latter lens, that is, the knowledge of the Absolute Self-Sufficient One, has been embedded at the end of the **Quran**, in the chapter *al-Ikhlas*.[6] It is the accentuation that the One denoted by the name **Allah** is **One** (*Ahad*) and **Absolute Self-Sufficient** (*Samad*). It is *HU*![7] There is no 'other' than *HU*! *As-Samad* connotes 'Absolute **Self-Sufficient ONEness to and from which nothing can be added or taken away.'**

If these two truths do not yield one view, **the soul of the Quran and the message it aims to give** can never be perceived correctly; the *reality* of the 'God up in the heavens and the prophet on earth' will never be known.

---

[6] *Al-Ikhlas*, literally means 'sincerity' in English, and is the name of the last and also the shortest chapter of the Quran.

[7] The Arabic word *HU*, though generally translated simply as 'He' is a reference made to the Absolute Essence as He Himself, His very Being, beyond description or comprehension, free of gender, superior to anything that can be conceptualized and far from any similitude whatsoever.

Indeed, this book endeavors to aid the reader to evaluate the signs of the Quran in the light of the One denoted by the name Allah, as the Absolute Self-Sufficient One.

As far as we are aware, there are no other works to the likes of this book. Many works have been produced conveying somewhat depthless and perhaps historical narrations of the Quran, rather than reflecting its actual message and soul. Most of these works employ such obscure language that it is no wonder many readers find it distasteful to read. Pedantic attempts to remain faithful to 'word-for-word' translations have reduced this **timeless literary masterpiece** into the misunderstood puzzle of our day.

Moreover, as you will see while reading it, this **literary masterpiece** frequently employs **various examples and metaphors** to explain the many truths contained within it, urging the reader to contemplate on their meanings... Sadly, however, the limited comprehension of the majority has taken these Quranic metaphors **literally** and rendered them as **laws**, fortifying their belief in a heavenly God, his messenger on earth and a heavenly book containing his decrees.

I am of the belief that if the essential idea can be duly reflected to the reader, people will have an exceedingly different approach and understanding of this supreme **knowledge**.

Due to this, before you start to **READ** it, I would like to share the principal message and some of the concepts of this **book – knowledge** according to my understanding.

The essential objective of the Quran is to aid the people to understand and get to know **the One denoted by** the name **Allah**, and to safeguard them against the God notion that leads to **duality** (*shirq*).

While believing in an external God, no matter how far and beyond in space He may be, is an explicit advocacy of duality (*shirq*), fostering ideas that there are 'other' beings with power in existence aside or apart from Allah (including one's ego) is an implicit promotion of duality.

The **knowledge** (Book) that has descended to address **humanity** forewarns its evaluators with these words:

"**Those who support 'duality'** (fragmenting existence; assuming there is a God *AND* there is everything *ELSE*) **are contaminated!**"

"**Those who have not cleansed themselves of the contamination** (of duality; the idea that there is a God and there is *also* me) **shall not touch it** (the knowledge – Quran… for they cannot understand it!)"

"**Indeed, duality** (assuming the existence of 'others' that are 'apart' from the One denoted by name Allah) **is a grave atrocity!**"

"**Duality is the only offence that Allah will definitely not forgive; everything else may be forgiven if He wishes to!**"

Those who want to be free of **duality** are encouraged to believe in the One denoted by the name Allah.

The Quran explains the two stages of believing in Allah as:

A) **To believe in Allah** (including faith in Allah with duality)

B) **To believe in Allah in accord with the meaning of the letter 'B'.**

The former elucidates the need to cleanse from the **explicit** notion of **duality** resulting from the illusion of an **external God.**

The latter, entails the pure belief that is free of even **implicit duality** which is the covert tendency of doing *shirq* by **equating one's ego or assumed self to one's *Rabb*** (the *al-Asma*, i.e. the Reality of the Names that constitute one's essential Reality).

Let us see how the paramount **knowledge of reality** revealed through **Sufism** (*tasawwuf*), to which many people scoff at, explains the misconception of **implicit duality** and how this topic is covered in the **Quran:**

This is directly from Hamdi Yazir's[8] translation. Notice that the verse isn't addressing the past, but it is talking directly to Rasulullah Muhammad (SAW) about the faith of the people around him at that time:

---

[8] The International Sahih translation has been used here.

"That is from the news of the unseen which We reveal, [O Muhammad], to you. And you were not with them when they put together their plan while they conspired.

And most of the people, although you strive [for it], are not believers.

And you do not ask of them for it any payment. It is not except a reminder to the worlds.

And how many a sign within the heavens and earth do they pass over while they, therefrom, are turning away.

And most of them believe not in Allah except while they associate others with Him." (Quran 12:102-107)

Now, let's remember the very important verse and warning that made me write the book *Mind and Faith* – Chapter 4 (*Nisa*), 136th verse is revealed to Muhammad (SAW) and is in reference to the believers around him:

'O you who have believed; *Aminu B'illahi'* **That is, 'O you have believed, believe in Allah in accord with the meaning of the B sign.'**

What does this mean?

It means: **Among all the worlds that are constituted by the meanings of the names of Allah, your reality, existence, and being also comprise the Names of Allah. Your** *Rabb***, your very Reality is the** *al-Asma* **(the Names). Therefore, neither you nor anything else around you is anything other than the manifestations of these Names. So do not be of those who fail to see this non-dual reality, and who give a separate existence to things** (like God) **they believe is 'other' than Allah. Such duality will only result in burning, both in this life and the next.**

However, the 8th verse of the 2nd Chapter (*Baqarah*) asserts the inability of the masses to conceive such truths as their manifestation (as the composition of the Names) is not as intellectuals:

"And of the people are some who say, 'We believe in Allah (in accord with the meaning of the B sign) **and the Last Day,' but they are not believers** (in accord with the meaning of the B sign).**"**

Hence, dismissing the eminent meaning entailed by the letter **B** simply as 'implicit duality' and not giving it the attention it deserves, has inevitable spawned the '*God up in the heavens, and me on earth*' misconception, resulting at the point it has come to today.

Whereas...

The invalidity of duality has been made evident right from the very first letter; the letter **B**, of the first verse (chapter) called the '***Basmalah.***' This truth, concealed by many Quran scholars due to the conditionings they receive throughout their training, was first made apparent by Hadhrat **Ali** approximately 1400 years ago.

Hadhrat Ali, the zenith of sainthood, pointed to this truth, considered to be a secret in his time, with his words:

"The secret of the Quran is in al-Fatiha (the opening chapter), the secret of al-Fatiha is in the B-ismillah, and the secret of the B-ismillah is in the letter B (ب). I am the POINT beneath the 'B' (ب)!"

This truth to which Hadhrat **Ali** was pointing, plays a key role in the Quran as a symbol of warning, initially encountered as the letter **B**, the first letter of the first verse '***B-ismillah***', and then throughout the whole Quran.

The late Hamdi Yazir, in his *Interpretation of the Quran*; Ahmed Avni Konuk, in his construal of the *Fusus-al Hikam* (*The Bezels of Wisdom* by Ibn Arabi) and Abdulaziz Majdi Tolun, in his commentary on *Insan-i Kamil* (*The Perfect Man*) have all given adequate warnings about this truth.

I, too, to the best of my capability, tried to evaluate the verses of this divine book in the light of this truth; taking into special consideration where the letter **B** has been used and what meaning it entails in this particular position.

The verse '***B-ismillah***' emphasizes the importance of **READ**ing the **Quran** with the awareness of the meanings implied by the letter **B**. The letter **B** points to the reality that, all joy or grief that is experienced by one, result from one's own inner reality, in accordance to the meanings projected from one's essence. The letter **B** tells us that one's experience of heaven or hell **is the direct result of one's actions**; that is, what manifests through one is based on the

Names that are inherent within them. Thus '***B-ismillah***' is repeated at the beginning of every chapter, reminding us of this truth.

According to my understanding, '***B-ismillahirrahmanirrahim***' is a chapter in itself.

It is impossible to understand the **Quran**, without first comprehending the purpose, indicated by the Absolute Reality the name **Allah** denotes, which is based on the Quran itself, and the teachings of the most magnificent human to have ever lived on earth, **Muhammad Mustapha (SAW)**.

If this purpose is not recognized, the wrong approaches will be taken towards the Quran; as if it were a history book, a good virtue book, a social order book, or a book containing the knowledge of the universe, etc.

Whereas, the most prominent truth that stands out to the **READer** who has no prejudice or preconditions, are the **hints that enable one to abandon the dual view**, and the teachings of the ways in which the consciousness can be cleansed towards this reality. Humans, because of the way they have been created, are immortal beings! **They only taste death** and, by constantly experiencing new realms of existence (*ba'th*), they go on to live an eternal life!

Death is the doomsday of the person, where the veil of the body is lifted and the person observes their own reality, and then begins to live the consequences of how much they were able to use this reality during their earthly life. As you **READ** you will see the various depictions of this throughout the book.

Hence...

Humans must know and understand their own reality and live their life accordingly, so they can use the **potential** arising from their **Reality** and earn **heavenly** life... that is, of course, if their **Rabb (the Names that comprise their essence)** has enabled them to! The act of turning towards one's Rabb, should not be an external turn, but an internal one towards one's own Reality, which is what praying (*salat*) is – an inward turn towards one's own essence.

At this point we must take heed of the following:

According to my understanding (and as I tried to elucidate in my book *Renew Yourself* the structure I refer to as the 'universe within universes', in respect of its reality, is a **multidimensional single frame picture**, or, a '**singular holographic knowledge – an ocean of energy**' with all its dimensions. The whole of this ocean is contained in each of its drops. It is the quantum potential! As **Rasulullah** (SAW) declared with his words: "**The part mirrors the whole!**"

As I have tried to explain in detail in my book *Muhammad's Allah* there is no '**other**' (concept, content, or form) in existence that can be likened or equated in any way to the One denoted by the name **ALLAH**.

Due to this reality, all enlightened beings extending from the contemplation and observation chain of Hadhrat Ali and Hadhrat **Abu Bakr**, who was referenced in the Quran as '**the second of the two**' have all confirmed the same reality: "**There is only Allah, and nothing else!**" This is why observing and evaluating His universal perfection (*hamd*) **belongs** only to **Allah**! As there is no other, Allah is the evaluator of Himself!

Duality is an invalid and **illusory** notion!

Mankind arrives at this erroneous judgment with their **illusions**, becoming veiled (*kufr*) to the **true Unity behind the misperception of multiplicity**! Consequently, people live their lives believing themselves to be **only the material body** which will eventually die and be cast away to nonexistence or they assume the existence of an exterior God, whether up in the heavens of within the self (*shirq*)!

Whereas according to the **people of Allah**, who base their views on the **Quran** and **Rasulullah**, the core of the matter is:

'**HU,' other than whom nothing exists, observes His knowledge, with His knowledge, i.e. the properties** (quantum potential) **denoted by the Beautiful Names** (*al-Asma al-Husna*), **in His knowledge** (the dimension of knowledge)... This act of observing has neither beginning nor end. **HU** is beyond being conditioned or limited by what He observes (i.e. HU is *Ghani* from the worlds.)

Hence, **all the worlds and everything they comprise**, which were all once **nonexistent** have become **existent** with the qualities of the **Names**, via this act of **observing**!

All things in the conceptual world are like the manifestations of the various compositions of the **Names of Allah**, shortly referred to as **the Names** (*al-Asma*). Just like how the approximately 100 hundred atoms comprise the whole of the material world with all its countless forms and beings.

Perhaps we can even say, the timeless, non-local quantum potential is **observing** itself from the point of view of the Names. Hadhrat **Ali**'s WARNING, "**Knowledge was a single point, but the ignorant have multiplied it**" denotes the reality that the **quantum potential** is a single **point**, which manifests into the perceived according to the perceiver, whereby these perceivers are the **ignorant**.

Albeit the **Beautiful Names** have generally been taught to be 99 in the broad sense, in respect of their details they are infinite.

All perceivable and non-perceivable things are made up of these **qualities that are denoted by the Names** (of Allah); hence, this act of creation has been referred to as '**the *Rabb* of the Worlds**.' The word '***Rabb***' is the **Name-composition** that constitutes the perceived individual.

The phrase '***bi-izni Rabb***' which literally means 'with the permission of *Rabb*' refers to the **suitability of the Name-composition to that particular situation.**

The phrase '***bi-iznillah***' which means 'with the permission of Allah' can denote either of two meanings, depending on its context. That is, it either refers to the **suitability and appropriateness of the Name-composition to the purpose of creation of the worlds**, or **the suitability of the Name-composition to the purpose of the individual's existence**. As there is no 'other' *Uluhiyyah* but the **ONE**.

Due to this **ONEness**, the **Quran** emphasizes the concept of **consequence** (*jaza*) and reinforces that all individuals will live the **consequences** of the behaviors that result from them. This is why there is a reiteration of the fact that '**each will live the consequences** of his or her actions, for there is no God that oppresses and punishes' throughout the Quran.

The meaning of 'all individuals will be given their due rights' means, whatever is necessary for the fulfillment of the individual's purpose of existence will be given accordingly.

Taqwa is generally understood as **protection** or 'to be protected from the wrath of Allah.' What this alludes to in fact is the protection one should take to avoid engaging in the behaviors that may result in the unfavorable expressions of the Names with which they have been created, as everyone will inevitably live the consequences of their own doings.

As I said, the **Quran** is not literally a written book sent down from God above to his postman-prophet on earth via certain intermediary beings. **It is the KNOWLEDGE of the Reality and the System (*Sunnatullah*), revealed (dimensionally) to his consciousness, from his *Rabb*, that is, the Names comprising his essential reality.**

In the view of the enlightened ones the Quran is a 'confirmation' in the appearance of a 'proposal.'

The BOOK alludes to the KNOWLEDGE pertaining to the Reality and the System (*Sunnatullah*).

In terms of being the **Knowledge of Reality** it reveals the **Reality** of everything, both perceivable and unperceivable. In terms of being the **Knowledge of the System** (*Sunnatullah*) it explains **the mechanics of the System and the Order of the dimensions in which individual beings will forever reside.**

A **human** is a **vicegerent** on earth. This can be understood both as the planet and as the body. For human is beyond a mere body, and once a human leaves the body, an indefinite continual of existence will go on through various forms of resurrections (*ba'th*).

All of the proposals that are made to humans are aimed at enabling them to know their true selves in the light of their Reality and to live the requirements of this, discovering and using their intrinsic qualities. All of the prohibitions, on the other hand, are essentially to prevent humans from being

deluded into thinking they are their physical body, and hence, squandering the potential given to them on egoistic, bodily pleasures that will have no meaning after they taste death. As their current potential has been given to discover their Reality and attain the beauty of both this life and the next.

If this work aids in a better evaluation of the **Quran**, I confess my inability to duly give thanks for such a blessing. My works are the compulsory requirement of my servanthood. Success is only with Allah's favor and blessing! I also apologize for my inadequacies and mistakes. For it is impossible for a servant to deservedly evaluate the words of Allah!

AHMED HULUSI
25 October 2008
North Carolina, USA

2

AN IMPORTANT NOTE ABOUT
UNDERSTANDING 'DECODING THE QURAN'

The Quran is the **knowledge** (book) revealed by the *presence of Allah*. No words or literal concepts pertaining to the 'presence of Allah' can be valid. Perhaps we may refer to the original of the Quran as being written in the language of **Allah**. For, if (as the Arab polytheists claimed) Muhammad (SAW) had written the Quran, then we could have said the Quran has been originally written in the Arabic language!

Whereas the Quran, originally in the language of Allah, was *revealed* by the angel Gabriel, to Muhammad (SAW), in his own language, Arabic, so that the people of that region can understand its message.

The Quran refers to this truth with the verse:

"And We did not send any Rasul except [speaking] in the language of his people to state clearly for them, and Allah [thereby] sends astray whom He wills and guides whom He wills. And He is *al-Aziz, al-Hakim*." (Quran 14:4)[9]

As the Quran, **originally in the language of Allah**, has been revealed in the very rich language of Arabic, it exposes different

---

[9] The Sahih International Quran.

levels of knowledge to different levels of understanding. Each verse, in respect of the metaphors and allegories it contains, signifies a various number of meanings.

Due to this profound depth contained in the original Quran that has been revealed to us in Arabic, it is impossible to duly and comprehensively translate (and interpret) this magnificent book into another language!

All translations and interpretations are limited by the knowledge and understanding of the translator's vocabulary. Hence, all such works are like excerpts from this magnificent source of knowledge.

At this point I'd like to draw your attention to an important detail.

Many Sufi scholars, also considered to be 'Saints', from Haji Baktash Waliyy to Muhyiddin ibn al-Arabi, spoke **flawless Arabic** and arrived at the same understanding based on the knowledge they gained from the Quran… On the other hand, followers of orders such as **Wahhabism**, who consider Muhyiddin ibn al-Arabi and the Sufi tradition to be blasphemous, *also* possess an **immaculate understanding of the Arabic language** and arrive at their judgment based on the *same* Quran.

Think about it!

How did the eminent scholars and saints, who had profound knowledge of the Arabic language, such as Abdul Qadir Jilani, Imam Ghazali, Sheikh Naqshbandi, Abdul Karim al-Jili, Syed Ahmad Rufai and Imam Rabbani, understand and apply the Quran? And how others, who also speak perfect Arabic and who claim these saints are **blasphemous (*kafir*)**, have arrived at *their* understanding of *a God, who apparently has hands and feet, who sits on a throne in heaven, and sends books down to Earth to guide humanity*!?

Sadly, many of the current translations of the Quran, especially the English ones, have been translated based on this latter understanding, while only a *rare few* works have been done in the light of the former approach.

This *Key to the Quran* may perhaps be considered more as a **figurative interpretation**. As far as I am aware it is the first of its kind in Turkey. It can never be considered to contain all of the meanings of the Quran. According to my observation, it may only be considered as reflecting only one of the many facets of this noble book. Another construal could have also been done, if it was desired, exposing other facets of the Quran.

Due to this reason, NO translation or interpretation of the Quran could be referred to as the 'Turkish Quran' or the 'English Quran'. One should read these books with the awareness that they are only vehicles to help one understand the Quran.

3

DECODING THE QURAN

The world has entered the Age of Aquarius declaring: **The time for renewal is upon us!**

Heeding this announcement, I too have renewed my outlook on the Quran, and have begun to approach it with a totally new understanding!

The warning in this **miraculous Book of Knowledge, "You say you follow in the footsteps of your forefathers, but what if your forefathers were on the wrong path?"** compelled me to re-evaluate the Quran from the very beginning with a completely new outlook.

Religion has become contaminated with outdated interpretations of the past and degenerated with stories from the corrupted version of the Old Testament, further reducing and simplifying it for the masses to understand. I knew beyond doubt that the reality of religion could only be reached through the correct understanding of the Quran.

So, on the 15th night of the month of Ramadan, I commenced my mission to decipher and share this knowledge with my brothers and sisters. I thoroughly studied the Quran in light of the well heeded guidance of eminent saints and scholars, such as Abdul Qadir Jilani, Muhyiddin ibn al-Arabi, Imam Rabbani, Ahmad Rufai, and Imam

Ghazali (may Allah's peace and blessing be upon them all). Thankfully, committing 15-18 hours a day, I was able to complete my study in 120 days. Thus emerged the understanding of the **Quranic verses** in respect of the meaning of the letter **B**.

Since the Quran addresses **the whole of humanity throughout all ages as guidance to the truth**, this particular construal has been done in the light of the realities of today, the modern age.

It is an explanation of why certain incidents that took place thousands of years ago, the details of which are unknown, have been narrated time and time again reaching us today, and possibly even the generations to come.

Most importantly, it employs a holistic approach to the seemingly disconnected events, laws, edicts and *commands of God,* **integrating** this miraculous **knowledge,** to define just *how* and *why* it is a concern to **humans**.

Let us now delineate our findings, some of which have been included in our work.

The Quran has come to man to inform them of the reality of their essence and what they will be faced with in the future, so they can observe certain practices and abstain from others accordingly.

What is the reality of **a human being**? Why did the Quran come to **remind – invoke** (*dhikr*) mankind of their reality?

The answers to these questions, along with how **man** should understand the One denoted by the name **Allah**, are the most important and prominent topics covered in the Quran.

Let me approach this with the method of the Quran and explain with a parable. Think of a baby who is placed in a car at the time of birth and is brought up in this car until he is 40 years of age, never once leaving the vehicle. Until he is 40 years old he is consistently programmed with the conditioning *"you are this vehicle",* such that by this age he has absolute and doubtless belief in it. Imagine now, he is told, at the age of 40: **"You are not this vehicle, you are a human being, get out of this vehicle and be free!"** But alas! He has come to see the steering wheel, the gearstick, and the gas and brake pedals as his very organs! How, at this point, can he be 'reminded' of the reality that he is not this vehicle, but that he is a 'human being' who can live independently of this vehicle?

He must first believe in what is being told, and then he must follow the instructions that are given to him so he can be emancipated...

As I have tried to explain with this simple example, **Humans** are beings with pure universal **consciousness** who have opened their eyes in an **earthly** body, operated by an individual **consciousness**!

Their self, the **consciousness** that is the **Universal Intellect** (*Aql-i kull*), has become veiled during the course their life, and **human beings** began to think they are merely the decomposable biological body they occupy.

Thus it became imperative to *remind* **them** of their reality! That is, that they are not the decomposable biological body in which they are temporarily residing, but an ethereal being! A being that will **change dimensions, level by level**, *realizing its angelic properties*[10] with which it will experience the realm of paradise!

This is why Rasuls were manifested to remind (warn) *earthlings* of their **human** qualities. So that, **humans**, aware of their essential reality, can prepare themselves accordingly for the infinite existence awaiting them after their biological bodies return to the earth.

As for those who lack **human** qualities, they will deny their reality (*kafir*) and live their lives driven by their earthly and bodily desires, deprived of the expressions of pure consciousness. Consequently, they will continue their indefinite existence **fully aware** in the state described as **hell**.

Everything that has emerged from **nothingness** into this realm of multiplicity derives its **existence** from, and functions with the **Names of Allah**. As such, in respect of pure **consciousness, humans** who become aware of and live according to this reality are termed **vicegerents**.

The Quran refers to such blessed souls as the **'living'** and **'seeing'** ones. While contrarily, those who fail to recognize or deny their reality, are referred to as the **'non-living'** and **'blind'** ones.

---

[10] Quran 84:19

Humans who recognize and live accordingly to their reality, possess **angelic** properties in terms of the essence of pure **consciousness. Such humans are essentially comprised of the properties denoted by Allah's names.** As they manifest the meanings of these Names, in ways befitting true humans, the state referred to as **heaven** occurs. In other words, heaven is not an abode for *mere earthlings*, but a state of life for **humans** whose **angelic** qualities can become manifest. I earnestly hope this point is understood well.

All examples and events that are narrated in the Quran are for the sole purpose of enabling **humans** to remember their essential reality, to *know* themselves, and hence to make better use of their current lives.

One of the most important things that deserves attention in regards to the style of the Quran is:

Everything, that is, **the heavens, the earth and everything in between**, is formed by the properties known as the **Names of Allah.** Hence, all perceivable and unperceivable things are invoking (calling upon) the One denoted by the Name Allah, by means of their life and function. Therefore, everything, with its natural disposition, is in a state of **servitude to the qualities of the Names** that comprise its existence, i.e. to Allah.

Due to this, the word 'WE' is used frequently in the Quran, emphasizing the reality that just as **the 'meaning' aspect of creation has been created with the Names the 'action' aspect of creation also comes about with the properties of the Names.**

Thus, by saying 'WE', the actions arising from the seeming multiplicities are actually being referred to their rightful owner.

'The *Rabb* of the Worlds' (*Rabbul Alameen*) refers both to the existence comprised of the Names and the actual Names comprising it.

This being the case, the structural properties of the pre-eternal Names and their expressions, i.e. the cosmos, are in no other state but that of absolute servitude to Allah. Creation is in a constant act of invoking and remembering Allah, displaying Allah's knowledge and power, at all times. Allah informing mankind about this reality is nothing other than a confirmation. This is why Allah says 'WE' when referring to the Names.

This being said, in order to prevent one from conditioning or limiting Him with these meanings, the warning that **His Absolute Essence (*dhat*) is 'beyond and free (*ghani*) from the worlds'** is frequently made. Nothing in existence can be likened to or define His Absolute Essence.

This also means, **His 'governance of the worlds' is through the paths of each of His Names, whether these Names manifest under the name of astrology, or as the known and unknown life forms within the cosmos; whether one calls it consciousness, or forms of consciousness, invisible beings, or heaven and hell, all dimensions of existence are various ways of His governance.**

As for the real meaning of polytheism or **duality (*shirq*)**: one who fails to recognize the One denoted by the name Allah in all that is implicit and explicit (within the self and in the outer world) **as the manifestations of the Names** is defined as a polytheist or a dualist in the Quran. In other words, assuming a separate and equal[11] existence to the manifestations of Allah's Names is an act of fragmenting the Oneness of reality, and hence an act of advocating duality (*shirq*). That is to say, it is an act of committing *shirq* (assuming a separate existence) with the Names, to the Names.

As can be understood from above, Allah, who in respect of **His Absolute Essence** is **free from concepts such as duality and non-duality**, defines *shirq* to be a failure to recognize the true nature of existence. That is, when one fails to see that everything in manifestation is essentially comprised of the Names, one is assuming an equivalent existence to the Names, and this goes against the reality of non-duality. Hence, such a person falls short of truly understanding Allah and goes on living in an illusory world in his imagination.

---

[11] The original word that is used in the Quran is ***min dooni Allahi*** which means 'as equal' or 'equivalent to' referring to an existence that is 'other' than Allah. Whereas, Allah affirms that no other form of existence can be found outside of Allah as Allah encompasses the whole of existence. Thus, negating any possibility of the equivalence of other gods, lords, etc, the Quran uses the word ***min dooni Allahi***.

Denial (*kufr*) on the other hand, rests upon the false belief that none is governing the individualized consciousness other than itself. Restricting the infinite consciousness to an individualized manifestation by calling it **'I'** is a grave insult and limitation to the infinite qualities of the Names, which cannot be confined to a mere physical body. Such an attempt is termed denial (*kufr*) and is said to be going against the infinite qualities of the Reality of the Self, at least in terms of **faith**. Continual attempts in this way eventually lead one to confine the Self to the physical body alone, paving the path to pursuing a life of bodily pleasures, and adopting the view that **death** is *extinction* rather than a change of abode.

Hypocrisy is the lowest and densest state of the bodily life. A hypocrite (*munafiq*) is one who chooses not only to deny the Reality but also to take advantage of the believers for material benefits by *imitating* them! While even a dog approaches his owner for food with true sincerity and loyalty, a hypocrite lacks genuine intent and approaches others only with vested interests. The result upon realizing the truth of the matter is indefinite burning and no compensation.

Faith (*iman*) is the realization of consciousness, through the intellect, i.e. through analysis of various data, that beyond the seeming reality of forms and concepts lies infinity and it is this infinity that must be sought after. It is to know the 'I'ness as consciousness, which cannot be confined into a material form, and to strive in this path. The hadith **"He who lives by 'La ilaha illallah'**[12] **will assuredly enter heaven"** points to this truth. This is applicable for those who have not encountered a Rasul. Those who have encountered a Rasul, whether by person or by teaching, are bound to believe in the **Rabb of the Worlds** (the source of the infinite meanings of the Names), or **Allah,** in accordance to the teachings of the Rasul, by having faith in the Rasul.

I say "having faith in the Rasul" because by appearance a Rasul is also an earthling with a physical body, there is no apparent difference between a Rasul and other humans. Yet the difference lies in that a Rasul is the articulation of the Reality, which cannot be seen

---

[12] "There is no God. There is only Allah."

with the physical eyes but initially experienced only through having faith.

The Quran explains **faith in the One denoted by the name Allah** as being in two stages. The first stage pertains to an 'external' creator beyond the reach of individual consciousness, that is, a creator or 'the dimension of the Names' comprising infinite and illimitable qualities. This is the faith shared by the majority of believers, and in terms of its proceeds, enables one to live a life bearing a paradisiacal state of existence. The second stage applies to believers with a truly enlightened heart and who have reached the essence of faith. This is the faith implied by the letter **B**, which points to the truth that the reality of the **Self** is the qualities of the **Names**, and these qualities are and forever will manifest themselves. Hence, it calls the believer to awaken to the reality that through his own acts he is at all times invoking and serving Allah, and as such, observing and evaluating the universal perfection of Allah on worldly forms *(Hamd)* manifested by the name *al-Waliyy* **in his own being** (*bi-Hamdihi*).

'**To believe in the angels**' means to have 'faith in the potentials' arising from the Names. In other words, **angels** signify the various potentials that arise during the process of the Names becoming activated from their dormant states. Since what has come to be known as the world of multiplicity essentially comprises individualized manifestations of various Names, the higher (subtler) state of everything in existence is **angelic** *(malakiyyah)*... The difference lies not in whether this is present or not, but in whether this reality is recognized or at least, believed in or not. One who accepts himself only as an earthling through individual consciousness and who lacks **faith** will have grave difficulty recognizing and accepting this truth.

'**To believe in the Books-Knowledge**' is to have faith in the **knowledge** of Reality and the mechanics of the system - *Sunnatullah* imparted by the Rasuls and Nabis via a process known as **revelation**, that being the dimensional transferal (emergence) of this knowledge through pure consciousness.

Rasuls are the enlightened ones who acquire the Knowledge of Reality through pure consciousness (without the influence of their personal consciousness) from the Names and angelic potentials in their essence via **revelation** and who communicate these truths at the level of consciousness.

To believe in the **afterlife**, or an eternal life, is to know with conviction that the Self will not become extinct after losing its body during death, but that **death** is also an experiential reality. That is, when the physical-biological body is omitted a process called resurrection (*ba'th*) will take place, during which one will pass to another dimension of life with the **spirit body**, shared by other invisible beings and eventually continue its life in either of two dimensions known by various names.

When the letter **B** is used as a prefix to a word in regards to having faith, such as 'to believe in the hereafter' (*bil-akhira*) or afterlife, it points to the various stages of development the **Self** will indefinitely go through[13] in pursuit of self-actualization.

The concept of **'protection'** (*taqwa*) or **'to have fear of Allah'** is also generally misunderstood. Since the name Allah does not refer to an external God, the real reference is made to the Names and their governance. Allah created the worlds with the Names and governs it with the System known as *Sunnatullah*. The one law that most absolutely applies here is that of the Name *al-Hasib* inherent in one's **'Name composition'**, whereby one's experience of their latter stage is a result of their former stage. Simply put, whatever behavior one has at any given time whether it is an action or a thought, one will inescapably live its consequence at some point in their life. This has been expressed as **'the One who is swift at reckoning'** (*sari-ul-hisab*) and **'the One who responds to wrongdoing with severe punishment'** (*shadid-ul-ikab*).

Therefore, living in a system with caution and prudence has been termed as 'fearing Allah' or as 'protection' (*taqwa*). Since **'Sunnatullah = the System and mechanics of Allah'** is essentially the manifestation of the Names of Allah, it is not incorrect to refer to this as 'fear and protection from Allah' after all. As such, an act of ungratefulness to any being is an act of ungratefulness to Allah, and its consequence will be lived accordingly! This process is known as

---

[13] Quran 84:19

'*jaza*' (consequence). Hence, *jaza* is not really the result or punishment but the *automatic experience* of the *consequence* of an act.

The Quran invites its readers to contemplate through its innumerous parables and metaphors, all to remind (*dhikr*) humans of their own reality.

Unfortunately, due to the conditions of time and place, and the comprehension levels of the people, the examples that can be given are not many. Due to this, the limited number of objects that people do know of has been associated with various meanings over time, such that the same word has been used to refer to different things in different times, or to different specifications of the same thing. For example, while the Arabic word '**sama**' is seldom used to refer to the 'sky' or 'space' it is more commonly used in reference to the 'states of consciousness' or the 'intellectual activity in one's consciousness.' Another example is the word '*ardh*'. While infrequently used to refer to the earth, it is generally used to refer to the 'human body.' The human body is also denoted by other words such as '**an'am**' which means 'domestic animal' referring to the animalistic nature of mankind, i.e. eat, drink, sleep, sex etc., and '**dabbah**' which refers to the material and earthly make-up of the biological body. The word '**shaytan**' (satan) has been used to connote mankind's tendency to reduce and limit their boundless consciousness, in respect of their essential Name composition, to the base bodily state. The word '**mountain**' is also seldom used to denote what it actually means; while it is more commonly employed to imply the 'ego', the 'I' or 'I'ness. Also, when the word '*ardh*' is used in reference to the '**body**', the word '**mountain**' is seen to denote the '**organs**' of the body. For example, the verse '**the mountains walk but you perceive them to be still**' indicates the constant activity and renewal of our interior organs, which seem to be fixed like the mountains on earth.

The word '*zawj*' is also used in various contexts to mean different things. While its most common usage is to mean '**partner in marriage**' it has also seen to be used in the context of consciousness implying the partner or **equivalent of consciousness and the body that will fall into disuse at some point**. In fact, the 7th verse of chapter 56, *al-Waqi'ah*, states '*azwajan thalathah*' to mean **'three kinds'** not three wives!

If we evaluate the words of the Quran in a constricted literal sense and in reference to only one meaning, we will not only be doing grave injustice but also paving the pathway to the primitive belief that it is an obscure and inconceivable Godly book of commands!

Whereas the Quran is the articulation, through revelation, of the *Rabb* of the worlds (the source of the infinite meanings of the Names), giving us the knowledge about the system by which the implicit qualities of the Names manifest to create the explicit world. This is what **'religion'** is!

Man, in other words **'pure consciousness'**, is the *personified* Quran. Earthlings who believe themselves to be no more than their physical bodies have been called 'human beings' due to this universal consciousness present in their innermost essence. When units of consciousness (in earthly bodies) refuse to have faith in this, they are denying their innermost essence and reducing themselves to mere material existence. Hence, the Quran describes such people as **'they are like cattle, nay, they are even more astray (from being a human) in their way'**.[14] In other words, only the animalistic appetites of their physical bodies drive their lives. They deny the magnificent and superior qualities of their own reality and function only with the stimuli of the neurons in their intestines (the second brain), thereby reducing their lives to the animal – bodily state.

As for the frequent narrations of the lives and examples of Rasuls and Nabis in the Quran... All of these are also **examples of possible intellectual or physical errors humankind are prone to and should be cautioned against.** Nevertheless, such incidents have been lived by every human population of every century in one way or another!

In regards to the creation of Adam, the Quran says: **'Indeed, the example of Jesus to Allah is like that of Adam'**.[15] That is, in terms of his physical body, Adam was also born from a mother's womb. His body also went through all the common biological stages of

---

[14] Quran 25:44
[15] Quran 3:59

development. This has been explained through various metaphors. Besides all of this, however, what is really meant by 'Adam' is a human who has **consciously** recognized and accepted **all of the meanings of the Names** and thus deserved the title **'vicegerent'**. This is what truly matters. All the rest are details and probably even unnecessary, as it doesn't really matter from where and how the material body, which will eventually decompose back into simple matter under the earth, came about. Certain symbols and metaphors have been employed to imply his biological aspect was created from the earth's atomic constituent, like all other earthlings, but his biological body is of no relevance to what is really being denoted by this name. **'Adam', is 'pure consciousness', formed from nothingness,** and composed of (*'ja'ala'* not *'khaleqa'*) the qualities of the Names and designated as a 'vicegerent' (*khalifa*) on earth. It is a shame that many fail to understand this reality and spend their lives arguing over the creation process of his mortal biological body!

The satanic being referred to as **'Iblis'** has an interesting story. Iblis, while essentially a Name composition comprised of angelic qualities, displays an inadequate expression of the Names *al-Waliyy*, *al-Mumin* and *al-Hadi*. Due to his own inadequacy, he fails to recognize how profoundly the Names are manifested on the creation of supreme form (*'ahsani takwim'*). Hence, he evaluates Adam according to his apparent qualities and fails to see his superiority in terms of the Names and their expressions. Moreover, he assumes that accepting the superiority of Adam over his own creation will mean denying his own reality, since he too is created with and from the Names, and thus he refrains from prostrating. Evidently, **it is impossible for one to evaluate a quality that he himself lacks.**

Eventually this leads to pure consciousness in the form of Adam approaching the forbidden tree, i.e. becoming restricted by the requisites of the bodily life. This is also an interesting anecdote. *Satan convinces Adam to the 'wrong' according to his own 'right',* imposing the idea: "You have been created with the Reality of the Names, you cannot be restricted or conditioned by anything, you should do as you wish. If you don't eat from the forbidden tree, that is, if you don't live the requirements of the bodily life, you would be accepting limitation and thus denying your essential reality, thereby depriving yourself of immortality!"

Consequently, humanity at the level of the Inspiring Self (*nafs-i mulhima*), symbolized with the name Adam, becomes veiled from the **higher states of** pure **consciousness**, and falls to the bodily state of the Commanding Self (*nafs-i ammarah*), becoming conditioned by bodily needs. When this reaches the ultimate point of forgetting their own essence, the reminders and imparters of reality, i.e. Rasuls, become manifest, inviting mankind back to their essence, back to having **faith** in the higher states of **consciousness**.

When human beings, who are manifestations of Universal Pure Consciousness, begin to experience themselves as individualized conscious beings in this physical body, the struggle of this relationship with their 'partner' (body) and the battle to go back to their essential reality commences.

In short:

There are two types of consciousness. The first is the manifestation of the Names as a whole, to observe itself through the appearance of individualized compositions. This is the Universal Pure Consciousness. The second kind is the individual consciousness of each manifestation, formed by genetic inheritances, environmental conditionings and astrological influences. For the purpose of clarity in this book, we will refer to the second kind as 'consciousness' to avoid confusion. Consciousness is an output of the brain and hence confines itself to comprise only the body (humanoid). Consciousness uses the mind to evaluate ideas and to live accordingly. But the mind, pressured by the body's biological make-up, often malfunctions. As such, it is near impossible for the mind to find the Reality all on its own. Furthermore, the mind makes judgments based on sensory perception. This is why the mind is invited to 'believe', to have **'faith'** in what lies beyond its area of perception. For, the reality 'beyond' matter encompasses matter.

While the stories of **Abraham** (SAW) caution us from idolizing and deifying our exterior and interior faculties, i.e., the body and its components, the narrations about **Lot** (SAW) give examples of the felonious lives led by those who were captives of their bodily demands and sexuality. In the case of **Moses** (SAW) on the other hand, the emphasis is on the Pharaoh's claim to be God, warning us from the grave danger we may encounter in pursuit of getting to know our true selves.

When the fruit of reality manifests in one's consciousness, no matter how essentially true it may be to claim 'I am the Reality', it is ultimately only one compositional reflection of the infinite Names that compose one's essence! The whole of manifestation comprises the **compositional Name qualities**. Thus, even though by 'essence' everything obtains its life force from 'Allah' and everything is the 'Reality' **they are not the 'Rabb of the Worlds'** (the source of the infinite meanings of the Names), **that is, nothing that has become manifest in the apparent cosmos can be the 'source' and 'discloser' of the infinite and illimitable Names!** Nothing that has become manifest can be the 'Rabb' of other manifestations. Hence, the Pharaoh encountered what he did because of his ignorance to this truth. All those who aspire to attain and live the reality go through this perilous state, known in Sufism as the station of the Inspiring Self (*nafs-i mulhima*)! Resultantly, just when one is a step away from the Reality, one becomes seized by the idea with which Satan infused Adam: "Do not restrict yourself! Do as you wish, become limitless!", and falls into the dense and base pit of the bodily state, the station of the Commanding Self (*nafs-i ammarah*). This is why the Quran repeatedly narrates the story of Moses (SAW) and the Pharaoh.

The event known as **doomsday** (*qiyamah*) points to the **various experiences of one's consciousness during the process of death**. The imminent doomsday is one's personal death. For, with death, an unchangeable state of existence known as the afterlife commences. The global doomsday has been awaited for approximately 1400 years now, whereas all that has been said in reference to doomsday has direct pertinence to one's own death. While everyone has their own Savior (*Mahdi*), Antichrist (*Dajjal*) and Jesus (*Isa*), and is subject to the activities symbolized by these names throughout their whole lifetime, people ignorantly think 'doomsday' is only a galactic event involving the end of our solar system or the world, supposedly to take place at some time predicted by some people!

Unfortunately, the inability to comprehend the life period of hundreds of millions of years at the galactic level, and the attempt to evaluate time based on the data received from one's untaught environment, and the primitive understanding of a God with a magic wand, had led humanity to adopt an improper understanding of the doomsday explained in the Quran.

As for **heaven and hell**... The Quran makes a clear statement **"heaven as a parable (representation, similitude)"**[16] and thus makes it evident that all expositions of 'heaven' in the Quran are symbolic and metaphoric. It is quite challenging to both comprehend and talk about a state of existence in which the **'awakened' ones** will dwell, in congruence with the Power and other Name qualities they will be endowed with, and far from all bodily limitations. This is why **"Allah says: I have prepared for my pious servants that which no eye has ever seen, no ear has ever heard, and no human mind has ever conceived"**.[17]

Hell is most certainly an atrocious state of existence, in terms of the physical body one will assume in that environment. According to our observation it will be sustained in the Sun. I wrote about this in detail in my book *The Mystery of Man* in 1985. On the other hand, hell in respect of consciousness, which has a stronger emphasis in the Quran, is a far more dreadful torment: When one dies they will realize they have been endowed with the **qualities and potentials of the Names**, and have been given the most perfect opportunity to discover and manifest these during their earthly life. In the case that they squandered this chance by indulging in the physicality of things rather than internal values, they will feel an inexplicably tremendous remorse knowing they no longer have a chance to compensate. This burning will be the greatest hellfire one can experience!

As for the hellish state of existence while still on earth, it is when the consciousness confines itself to a bodily state of existence and becomes attached to others and conditioned by value judgments.

There are many more notes to make but I guess I should not extend this introduction any further. If the *Rabb* of the Worlds (the source of the infinite meanings of the Names), wills, the doors of inspiration will be opened up to you also and you will have the

---

[16] Quran 52:20 and 47:15, '*Math'alul jannatillatiy*'
[17] Bukhari Muslim and Tirmidhi

delightful experience of READing the **living Quran** as it talks to you in person, and tells you about yourself.

Nevertheless, if you read this work, *Decoding The Quran*, in light of all that I have explained here, I believe you will hear it talking to you and feel the Quran living within your Self in a way that you have never experienced before.

If you question my concept... All I can say is, let us wait and see... Death is too near! If I am rightly guided, it is with the favor of Allah, and I am forever impotent from duly thanking Him. If this work is valid and legitimate, I don't know how those with differing opinions will react! This is my understanding of the Quran, how you take it is up to you!

If, in this work that I share with you without any material expectation in return, any humanly interference has occurred on my part besides my *Rabb*'s (the Names constituting my essence) guidance and inspiration, I earnestly apologize.

All success is from Allah, and any shortcoming or error is from the inadequacy of my individual consciousness.

Astaghfir'ullah wa atubu ilayh[18].

AHMED HULUSI
21 January 2009
North Carolina, USA

---

[18] I ask for repentance (forgiveness, the covering of my shortcomings due to my human nature) from Allah. My repentance (return) is to HU alone.

4

AN ESSENTIAL MESSAGE

Unfortunately, my interpretation of the Quran, which has been done in the light of the **Knowledge of Reality**, has inadvertently led to some misunderstandings. One of these is the notion that everything begins and ends with man. Of course, in respect of man's essential reality, all that I have written are concepts that are shared by and agreed upon by all enlightened individuals.

However...

Mankind isn't the be-all and end-all.

We cannot deny that within the universe and galaxy in which we reside, in fact within our very solar system, exists countless different species of life forms, which our five-sense dependent science has not yet perceived, but which many unconditioned, objective people find very comprehensible.

The system mechanics that constitutes the make-up of a human being may very well be present in other species in the universe.

This truth is validated in the Quran!

Whether we take the example of **Abraham** (SAW), **Lot** (SAW) or even **Mary** (SAW) we repeatedly encounter these beings mentioned as **'Rasuls'** throughout the Quran.

Moreover, I may very comfortably state that the angelic being referred to as **'Gabriel'** is not a product of imagination but a form of life unable to be fully perceived by our limited sense perception, while its images are a product of the data processing system in the brain. This applies to all beings referred to as angels!

I do not feel it is appropriate to say anything further regarding this topic at this stage, when the intrinsic mechanics of the brain are only just being discovered and reported in our modern world. But I must add one more note: If you believe in their sincerity and genuineness, many enlightened saints such as Abdul Karim al Jili and Muhyiddin ibn Arabi have made contact with these life forms. The following thought provoking verse also pertains to this truth:

"I have no knowledge of the discussions of the *Mala-i Ala* (the Exalted Assembly of angels)."[19]

There are many reports regarding certain species and their functions referred to as '*Mala-i A'la*' in Shah Waliyyullah Dahlawi's renowned book *Hujjatullah Baligha*, translated into Turkish by the Theology Professor Hayreddin Karaman.

Rasulullah Muhammad's (SAW) words: **"Befriend me with the *Rafiq-i A'la*** (the Highest Company)"** also sheds light on this phenomenon!

Therefore...

One should not become so captivated with the inner dimension of things as to neglect their exterior-universal aspects.

Finally, as I had stressed in my book *Spirit, Man, Jinn* 40 years ago, let us be well aware and cautioned against the 'jinni activities' marketed today under the guise of being 'angelic.'

AHMED HULUSI
18 June 2010

---

[19] Quran 38:69

5

THE EXALTED, MAGNIFICENT AND PERFECT QUALITIES OF THE NAMES OF ALLAH (*AL-ASMA UL-HUSNA*)

B'ismi-Allah ar-Rahman ar-Rahim... Allah, who created me with His Names (exalted, magnificent, and perfect qualities), is *Rahman* and *Rahim*!

Let us heed the fact that a **'name'** is only used as a **reference** to an object or quality. A name does not explain what it references in totality, but merely alludes to an identity, or an attribute of an identity. Sometimes, a name is used only to channel the attention to multiple qualities, without revealing anything about the identity.

In the case of the **Names of Allah**, let us contemplate the following: Are the Names of Allah *a collection of fancy titles of a God beyond*? Or, are they references made to the creational properties of Allah (which the senses and conditionings externalize!) with which the entire known cosmos and everything in it becomes manifest from **nothingness** into a shadow **existence**?

Once this reality is fully conceived and comprehended we may move on to the Names of Allah.

The Quran, which has been conveyed as a *Dhikr*, i.e. 'the remembrance of man's essential reality', is actually a disclosure of the Names to expound '*Uluhiyyah*'. It is the **Totality of the Names** (all of the Names that have been imparted to us and that comprise our existence) that man has been endowed with and is invited to **remember**! Some of these have been disclosed in the Quran and some were revealed by the Rasul of Allah. One can never say that the names that refer to Allah are limited to only 99. Let us give an example... There are many names, such as *Rabb, Mawla, Kareeb* and *Hallaq*, that are mentioned in the Quran but are not included as part of the 99 Names. The name *Mureed*, which alludes to the attribute of '**will**' (i.e. He does as He wishes) mentioned in the verse '*yaf'alu ma yureed*', is also not included among the 99 Names. Contrarily, the names *Jalil, Wajid* and *Majid* are all included in the 99 Names but are not mentioned in the Quran. Thus, it would be a mistake to confine the Names of Allah to only 99, when the **Dimension of the Names** designates the infinite quantum potential, which involves the act of **observing in Allah's Knowledge**. Man is provided with these Names as a reminder of their own true essence. Perhaps once one remembers and lives accordingly to their essential reality, many more Names will be disclosed to them. Also, we may say **heaven** alludes to this truth too, while we may not even be aware of the Names that pertain to and compose the universes within universes of infinite existence!

The enlightened ones (*Ulul Albab*) have used the phrase '**the shadow existence**' to mean 'the things we perceive do not exist in and by themselves but they are compositions of Names that manifest **according to the perceiver**'.

In fact, even the phrase 'Name compositions' is metaphorical; it is only to adapt the dual view to the One reality. Absolute reality is the observing of the '**multidimensional single frame**' by the One who '**manifests Himself every moment in yet another wondrous way**'.[20] What we refer to as 'Name compositions' is only like one stroke of the paintbrush on this magnificent picture.

Due to having a **name** all perceivable things seemingly have a separate individual existence, whereas, because there is no God beyond, **what is really perceived as an existent object is**

---

[20] Quran 55:29

essentially none other than the materialized Names (qualities) of Allah.

This being said, the One denoted by the Names cannot be divided or fragmented into pieces, it is not composed of parts, it is even beyond concepts such as being 'absolute One', 'illimitable', 'infinite' and so on. It is *'Ahad-us-Samad'* (the Absolute Self-Sufficient One) and only mentioned this way in the Quran once! **Allah, HU, other than whom nothing exists!** This knowledge cannot be comprehended by the human mind unless it is revealed or divinely inspired and observed in one's consciousness! The mind, logic and judgment cannot survive here. He who attempts to intellectualize this reality will only be misguided. This reality is not open for debate! Any urge to do so will only reveal ignorance! This is the reality that pertains to Gabriel's words: **"If I take one more step I will burn"**!

It must be realized that the Names of Allah point to the quality of His knowledge, not His *mind*, as this is inconceivable. The **mind** is a function of the brain designed to create the world of multiplicity. Essentially, even the phrases 'the Universal Intellect' (*Aql-i kull*) and 'the First Intellect' (*Aql-i awwal*) are relative concepts and are used metaphorically to denote the system by which the attribute of **knowledge** is disclosed.

The Universal Intellect refers to the dimension of knowledge that is present within the depths of all beings, within one's essence. This is also the source of revelation.

The First Intellect, on the other hand, is a tailored phrase for the novice mind, to describe the dimension of knowledge present in the manifestation (*sh'an*) of the Names.

'The dimension of Acts' (*af'al*) is nothing but the disclosure of the Dimension of Names which 'manifests itself every moment in yet another wondrous way'! The material world as we know it is this quantal plane, though differences of perception have led to the assumption that it is a **different** dimension.

The observing One, the one being observed, the observation, are all ONE! 'The wine of paradise' alludes to this experience. One who is caught up in the perception of **multiplicity** has no chance but to engage in the chatter of this knowledge, without any experience of its reality.

As for the **Acts**, activities, multiplicity and what we perceive as the corporeal world... Existence belongs only to that which is denoted as the Dimension of Names.

'**Observing knowledge in knowledge with knowledge**' designates that the very disclosure of the Names is the act of **observing**. In this respect, all **forms** are created and observed in knowledge. Hence it has been said '**the worlds (or creation) have not even smelled the scent of existence yet**'. Here, the **part** is the observer, and the **whole** is the observed one!

The force (*kuwwa*) pertaining to the Names is referred to as **angels**, which, in essence, constitute the **reality of mankind**. One who becomes aware of their reality is said to have '**united with their *Rabb***'! Once this state is reached, if it doesn't continue, the resulting pain has been narrated as an intense hellish suffering! This is the domain of **Power** (*Qudrah*) and the command **Be!** (*Kun*) originates from here; this is the dimension of **knowledge**, where the mind and its functions are completely obsolete! This is the essence of the land of **wisdom** (*hikmah*)! The **mind** can only watch the activities that take place in the land of wisdom, where only **consciousness** can actively participate!

The dimension of Acts (*af'al*) in comparison to this plane (the dimension of Power) is a totally **holographic** (shadow) state of existence. All the activities of the entire parallel and multiple universes and all their inhabitants, i.e. natural resources, plants, animals (humanoids) and the jinni, are **governed** by the *Mala-i Ala* (the Exalted Assembly of angels) in this plane, depending on the perception capability of the perceiver.

Rasuls and their successors, the saints, are like the vocal expressions of the *Mala-i Ala*, that is, the forces (potentials) of the Names, on earth! And all of this is part of the **observation** taking place in the **dimension of Knowledge**! The essence of **man**, in this sense, is **angelic** and he is invited to **remember his angelic nature and to live accordingly**. This is an in-depth and intricate topic... Those who are not acquainted with this knowledge may find my words regarding the **observation** taking place from various dimensions to be contradictory. However, the reality I experienced when I was 21 years of age in 1966, which I have penned in my book *Revelations*, has been verified time and time again throughout the 45 years that followed it, and I have shared it all without expecting any tangible or intangible return. The knowledge I share is not a pass-down to me, rather it is the direct blessing of Allah for which I am eternally grateful! As such, there is no contradiction in my words. If it appears that way, it is probably due to the inability to make the correct connections, resulting from an inadequate database.

So, if this is the reality as I have observed, how should the topic of the **Names of Allah** be approached?

The Names of Allah are initially expressed through pure consciousness (revelation) without the interference of one's consciousness, which tries to evaluate them later. The Names are cosmic universal qualities (not in the galactic sense).

The Most Beautiful Names belong to Allah. The structural qualities they denote pertain to the Absolute Self-Sufficient One. The Names look to the quantum potential beyond time and place; the Names signify the **point**. As such, the Names and their meanings belong to Allah alone and are free from becoming conditioned by human concepts.

"Exalted (*Subhan*) is Allah beyond what they attribute [to Him]." (Quran 23:91)

"And to Allah belongs the best names, so turn to Him through the meanings of His names. And leave [the company of] those who practice deviation (fall into duality) **concerning His names. They will be recompensed for what they have been doing."** (Quran 7:180)

That is, leave the company of those who restrict the Names with their humanly values, and fail to recognize the reality of the Beautiful Names and who do not know Allah is respect of His *Akbariyyah*!

"And (he who) believes (confirms) the Most Beautiful (Names) (to be his essential reality) **we will ease him towards ease."** (Quran 92:6-7)

Even the consequence of **good** is related to the Names:

"For them who have done good (*ihsan*) is the Most Beautiful (Names) and more. No darkness (egotism) **will cover their faces** (consciousness)**, nor derogation** (which results from deviating from one's essence)**. Those are companions of Paradise; they will abide therein eternally."** (Quran 10:26)

Allah's Absolute Essence (*dhat*) cannot be likened to anything in existence. With His greatness (*Akbariyyah*) He is free from becoming limited or conditioned by His creation or the attributes denoted by His Names, which constitute one point amongst infinite others. In other words, what is referred to as the **Dimension of Names** is like a multidimensional holographic single frame. And, despite the fact that it is perceived as the **realm of multiplicity**, this realm of activity is essentially a unified field of existence created with the compositional qualities in His knowledge.

To summarize before going further…

The qualities and attributes that we have come to acquire through revelation as the Names of Allah (singular in nature) are the very structural compositions that manifest the totality of all the universal dimensions, from nothingness into this shadow (holographic) existence. This reality, of which earthly vicegerency aspires to become aware, is far beyond the reach of the cruel and ignorant.

The Dimension of Names is the 'exalted, magnificent, and perfect attributes and qualities' with all its sub-dimensions and inner-existence!

Let us now ponder on the world perceived by humanity… and then **"raise our gaze to the heavens and observe"** as the Quran states, without dogmatic views and bigotry, with the understanding of universality formed by proficient knowledge!

What value does a world based on our miniscule perception have in comparison to the magnificence, glory and perfection of the universe?

I hope, in the light of this understanding, we can approach the **Names of Allah** with the awareness that their revelation depends on the purging of the individual consciousness (based on its limited perception and conception of the Book of Knowledge) and that **their effects pertain to the whole of the cosmos**, constantly manifesting new meanings and expressions.

I would also like to take this opportunity to express one of my concerns. I do not feel the knowledge I shared through previous articles has been correctly understood. Let me restate that the meanings, qualities and attributes denoted by the **Names of Allah are only one point among infinite others in the sight of Allah**. Also, the quantum potential expressed as the **Reality of Muhammad** or the **Angel named Spirit** is not only pre- and post-eternal, but it is also the reality I refer to as the 'multi-dimensional single frame' picture! Because this has not been well understood, Allah is still perceived *as the one God out there*! Whereas the whole **observation** and all that has been articulated pertain only to a **point**: Allah is just Allah, Allah is *Akbar*! *Subhanahu min tanzihiy[21]*!

Please be aware that what I write and share with you can never be taken as the final conclusion; in fact, it can only be an introduction! It is not possible to openly disclose through publication matters that are deeper than this. Anyway, the people of this path will recognize that even what we have already shared are things that have never been shared in this much detail and this openly before. This is a very sensitive topic as the reader may very easily fall into the misconception of either an external God or worse, confine the reality to his Pharaoh-like 'I'ness and animalistic bodily self!

I tried to shed some light on the topic of the Names (*al-Asma*). Let us now take a look at the qualities and attributes denoted by these exalted, magnificent and perfect Names (*al-Husna*)… As much as simple words allow of course…

THE TRIGGER SYSTEM

All of the qualities and attributes pertaining to the Names are entirely present at every point of existence! However, depending on the desired manifestation, some attributes gain precedence over

---

[21] HU is beyond comparability!

others, like the channels in an equalizer, to make up the specific formation. Also, qualities denoted by **certain Names naturally and automatically trigger the expressions of certain other Names**, in order to generate a new manifestation. This system is known as '*Sunnatullah*' and entails the **universal laws of Allah** (or the laws of nature as those with limited perceptive ability would say) and the mechanics of His system.

This is a glorious mechanism beyond description; all beings from pre-eternity to post-eternity subsist with all their inter and inner dimensions and perceivable units within this system!

All **thoughts** and **activities** projecting from consciousness, whether through the universe or a single person's world, are all formed within and according to this system.

In short, we may refer to this mechanism, where qualities of Names trigger one another, as the **trigger system**.

As I warned above, consider the entire universality of existence (which is ONE by essence) as the plane of manifestation of these Names. The trigger system applies to every instance of perception by a perceiver in every plane of existence within this universality. Since the entire sequence of certain qualities triggering other qualities is a *known*, it is said that the pre- and post-eternal knowledge of everything that has and will happen at all times is present in Allah's knowledge!

The following verses and the Name *Hasib* allude to this trigger system:

"...Whether you show what is within your consciousness (your thoughts) **or conceal it, Allah will bring you to account for it with the Name *Hasib*..."** (Quran 2:284)

"So whoever does an atom's weight of good will see it." (Quran 99:7)

Evidently, the consequence of an action or thought is inevitably experienced within this system. **This is why every thought or action of gratitude or ungratefulness we may have output in the past would have most definitely caught up with us, or is bound to in the future.** If one seriously contemplates on this many doors will open and secrets will reveal themselves. The **mystery of fate** is also pertinent to this mechanism!

Let us now follow these signpost-like Names to discover the secret lands they point to:

ALLAH

ALLAH... Such a name... It points to *Uluhiyyah*!

Uluhiyyah encompasses two realities. HU which denotes **Absolute Essence** (*dhat*) and the realm of infinite points in which every single point is formed by the act of **observing knowledge through knowledge**. This act of observing is such that each point signifies an individual composition of Names.

By respect of His absolute essence, Allah is **other than**, but in terms of His Names, Allah is the **same as** the **engendered existence** (*sh'ay*) yet nevertheless **far and beyond** (*Ghani*) **from the worlds and any similitude!** This is why Allah, who created the engendered existence (*sh'ay*) and the acts with His Names, uses the plural pronoun 'We' in the Quran. For, in essence, the engendered existence (everything in creation) is none other than Allah! Please note that by engendered existence (*sh'ay*) we are referring to the Dimension of Names that constitute existence. One can ponder and contemplate the essence of creation and existence, but **one cannot contemplate the Absolute Essence of Allah**. It is inconceivable and inappropriate; indeed, it is absolutely impossible! This is because one that has been created with the expressions of Allah's Names cannot fully comprehend the Absolute Essence of Allah! Even if this knowledge is revealed by **divine inspiration** – which is impossible – it is inconceivable. This is why it is said 'the path of such pursuit ends in nothingness'.

HU

HU'Allahulladhiy la ilaha illa HU!

Whether via revelation or through consciousness, HU is the inner essence of the reality of everything that is perceived... To such extent that, as the reflection of *Akbariyyah*, first **awe** then **nothingness** is experienced and, as such, the Reality of Hu can never be attained! **Sight cannot reach HU!** HU denotes absolute obscurity and incomprehension! As a matter of fact, all names, including Allah are mentioned in connection with HU in the Quran!

"HU ALLAH is AHAD."

"HU is RAHMAN and RAHIM."

"HU is AWWAL, AKHIR, ZAHIR and BATIN."

"HU is ALIY and AZIM."

"HU is SAMI and BASIR."[22]

And also the last three verses of Chapter *al-Hashr*...

It is also important to note that using HU as a prefix to other Names is first to establish incomparability (*tanzih*) and then to denote similarity (*tashbih*) in reference to the given Name. This should be remembered at all times.

AR-RAHMAN

Ar-Rahman signifies the materialization of the essence of every iota, with Allah's Names in His knowledge. In modern terms, it designates the quantum potential. It is the potential of the source of the entire creation. It is the name of the **Dimension of Names!** All things obtain their **existence** at the level of **knowledge and will** with the attributes denoted by this name.

As signified by the verses *"ar-Rahmanu ala'l arsh'istiwa"* (Quran 20:5)[23] and *"ar-Rahman Allamal Quran, Khalekal Insan, Allamul*

---

[22] The definitons of these Names are in the following pages.

[23] *Rahman* is established on the Throne (*Rahman* established His sovereignty by creating the worlds with His Names, i.e., *Rahman* observes His knowledge with His knowledge, in the quantum potential.

bayan" (Quran 55:1-4)[24]. *Rahman* is the reality that manifests in **consciousness**! The 'mercy' is in the act of 'manifesting it into existence.'

The narration of Muhammad (SAW) that **'Allah created Adam in the image of *Rahman*'** means the knowledge aspect of man reflects the qualities of *Rahman*, i.e. the qualities of the Names.

The essence (*dhat*) of man is also related to the name *Rahman*. As such, the polytheists are not able to comprehend the notion of prostrating to *Rahman* (Quran 25:60) and Satan (the mind, illusion) rebels against *Rahman* (Quran 19:44). These verses indicate the manifestation of the essence of 'Man'.

AR-RAHIM

Ar-Rahim is the name that brings the infinite qualities of *ar-Rahman* into engendered existence. In this sense, it is the 'observation' of the potential. *Ar-Rahim* observes itself through the forms of existence, by guiding the conscious beings to the awareness that their lives and their essential reality are comprised of and governed by the Names.

"...And ever is He, *Rahim* to those who believe in their essential reality" (Quran 33:43).

Ar-Rahim is the source of the plane of existence referred to as 'heaven'.

Ar-Rahim is the producer of the angelic state.

AL-MALEEK

The Sovereign One, who manifests His Names as he wishes and governs them in the world of acts as He pleases. The one who has providence over all things.

"So exalted (*Subhan*) is He in whose hand (governance) is the *Malakut* (the force of the Names) of all things, and to Him you will be returned." (Quran 36:83).

---

[24] *Rahman*, taught the Quran, created man, and taught him eloquence.

The Sovereign One who has no partners!

He who is blessed with this awareness will find himself only in absolute submission to *al-Maleek*! Objection and rebellion will cease. *Al-Maleek* is the foremost quality pertinent to the phenomenon known as its manifestations through a continuum (*arsh-i istiwa*).

"Whatever is in the heavens and whatever is on the earth is exalting (with their unique dispositions) **Allah, al-Maleek, al-Quddus, al-Aziz, al-Hakim** (to manifest whatever meanings He desires)." (Quran 62:1)

AL-QUDDUS

The One who is free and beyond being defined, conditioned and limited by His manifest qualities and concepts! Albeit the engendered existence is the disclosure of His Names, He is pure and beyond from becoming defined and limited by them!

AS-SALAM

One who enables a state of peace by emancipating individuals from the conditions of nature and bodily life and endows the experience of 'certainty' (*yakeen*). One who facilitates the comprehension of Islam for the believers, and enables the heavenly state of existence called '*Dar'us-Salam*' (the explicit manifestation of our implicit potentials).

This name is triggered by the name *ar-Rahim*:

"[And] *Salam* **a word from a *Rahim* Rabb.** (They will experience the manifestation of the name *Salam* from their *Rabb*, which is the reality of the Names comprising their essence)[25]."

---

[25] Quran 36:58

AL-MU'MIN

The One who enables the awareness that He, by respect of His Names, is beyond what is perceived. This awareness reflects upon us as **'faith'** (*iman*). All believers, including Rasuls and angels, have their faith rested upon this awareness, which frees the mind from the enslavement of illusion. While illusion can deter the mind, which uses comparison to operate, it becomes powerless and ineffective in the sight of faith.

The inherent quality of the Name *al-Mu'min* manifests itself directly from Awareness in one's consciousness, thereby rendering obsolete the effect of illusion.

AL-MUHAYMIN

The One who maintains and protects the manifestations of His Names with His own system (*al-Hafidhu war-Rakiybu ala kulli shay*)!

Al-Muhaymin also designates the One who safeguards and protects (the trust).

The root word of *al-Muhaymin* is *amanah* (trust), mentioned in the Quran as the trust from which the heavens, the earth and the mountains refrained, but which 'Man' (the twin brother of the Quran) accepted. Essentially, it indicates the consciousness pertaining to the knowledge of the Names, symbolized as the angel 'SPIRIT', which is then passed on to Man, the vicegerent on earth. That is, the 'trust' signifies living with the awareness that your essence is comprised of the Names. This works in conjunction with the name *al-Mu'min*. The angel (force) named SPIRIT also possesses a form since it is also a manifestation, and as such, it is *Hayy* and *Qayyum* due to the perfection of its 'faith' in the infinite qualities of the Names.

AL-AZIZ

The One who, with His unchallengeable might, disposes as He wishes. The One whose will to do as He likes, nothing can oppose.

This name works in parallel with the name *Rabb*. The *Rabb* attribute carries out the demands of the Aziz attribute!

AL-JABBAR

The One whose will is compelling. The corporeal worlds (engendered existence) are compelled to comply with His demands! There is no room for refusal. This *'jabr'* (compelling) quality will inevitably express itself and apply its laws through the essence of beings.

AL-MUTAKABBIR

The One to whom the word 'I' exclusively belongs. **Absolute 'I'ness** belongs only to Him. Whoever, with the word 'I', accredits a portion of this Absolute 'I'ness to himself, thereby concealing the 'I'ness comprising his essence and fortifying his own relative 'I'ness, will pay its consequence with 'burning' (suffering). Majesty (Absolute 'I'ness) is His attribute alone.

AL-KHALIQ

The ONE Absolute Creator! The One who brings individuals into the existence from nothingness, with His Names! Everything *al-Khaliq* creates has a purpose to fulfill, and according to this unique purpose, possesses a natural predisposition and character. Hence it has been said: **"characterize yourselves with the character of Allah"**[26] to mean: Live in accordance with the awareness that you are comprised of the structural qualities of the Names of Allah!

AL-BARI

The One who fashions all of creation (from micro to macro) with unique functions and designs yet all in conformity with the whole, like the harmonious functioning of all the different organs in the body!

---

[26] *'Tahallaku biakhlakillah'*

AL-MUSAWWIR

The fashioner of forms. The One who exhibits 'meanings' as 'forms' and devises the mechanism in the perceiver to perceive them.

AL-GAFFAR

The One who, as requisites of divine power or wisdom, 'conceals' the inadequacies of those who recognize their shortcomings and wish to be freed from their consequences. The One who forgives.

AL-QAHHAR

The One who executes the effects of His Name '*Wahid*' and renders invalid the seeming existence of the relative 'I'ness.

AL-WAHHAB

The One who bestows and gives unrequitedly to those He wishes, oblivious of deservedness.

AR-RAZZAQ

The One who provides all necessary nutrition for the survival of any unit of manifestation regardless of its plane of existence.

AL-FATTAH

The One who generates expansion within individuals. The One who enables the recognition and observation of Reality, and hence, that there is no inadequacy, impairment, or mistake in the engendered existence. The One who expands one's vision and activity, and enables their proper usage. The One who enables the recognition and use of the unrecognized (overseen).

AL-ALEEM

The One who, with the quality of His knowledge, infinitely knows everything in every dimension with all its facets.

AL-QABID

The One who exercises His verdict by retaining the essence of an individual's Name reality. The One who restrains and enforces withdrawnness.

AL-BASIT

The One who opens and expands; the One who enables dimensional and in-depth sight.

AL-KHAFID

The One who abases. The One who capacitates a state of existence which is far from reality. The creator of the *'asfali safileen'* (the lower state of existence). The former of the vision of **'multiplicity'** to conceal the reality.

AR-RAFI

The One who exalts. The one who elevates conscious beings to higher states of existence; to enable the realization and observation of their essential reality.

AL-MU'IZZ

The Giver of Honor. The One who bestows honor to whom he wishes and holds them in esteem over others.

AL-MUDHILL

The One who exposes dishonor in some and degrades below others. The One who deprives from honorable qualities and compels to humiliation with the veil of 'I'ness (ego).

AS-SAMI

The One who perceives His manifestations at every instance. The One who enables awareness and comprehension.

This name triggers the Name *al-Basir*.

AL-BASIR

The One who is constantly observing His manifestations and evaluating their outputs.

AL-HAKAM

The Absolute Judge whose judgment (verdict) is irresistibly applied.

AL-ADL

The One who provides each of His manifestations their due right in consonance with **their creation program**. The One who is absolutely free from unjustness or tyranny.

AL-LATIF

The One who is subtly present in the depths of every manifestation. The One whose favors are plentiful.

AL-HABIR

The One who is aware of the manifestations of His Names at all times. The One who allows his manifestations to discern the level of their comprehension via their outputs.

AL-HALIM

The One who refrains from giving sudden (impulsive) reactions to events, but rather evaluates all situations in respect of their purpose of manifestation.

AL-AZIM

The magnificent glory beyond any manifestation's capacity of comprehension.

AL-GHAFUR

The One who's Mercy should never be doubted or given up on. The One who enables necessary cleansing and triggers the name *Rahim* to bestow blessings.

ASH-SHAKUR

The One who allows the proper use of His bestowals in order that He may increase them. The One who enables the due evaluation of resources such that more can be attained. This name triggers the name *al-Karim*. If this name is not activated in one's life, one will be obstructed from a connection with Allah and not able to duly use his resources, turning his attention to other things and hence becoming veiled from the blessings of Allah. This leads to 'ungratefulness', which is defined as the inability to adequately evaluate and use blessings. Eventually this results in total deprivation.

AL-ALIY

The Highest (or the Sublime). The sublime One who observes existence from the point of reality (essence).

AL-KABIR

The magnitude of the worlds He created with His Names are incomprehensible.

AL-HAFIZ

The One who provides all requirements to preserve and maintain existence.

AL-MUQEET

The One who facilitates the expression of the Name *al-Hafiz* by providing the necessary material and spiritual platform for it.

AL-HASIB

The One who maintains individuality by holding them to account of their behavioral output through the mechanics of 'consequence'.

In doing so, an indefinite flow of formation is established.

AL-JALIL

The One who, with His magnificent comprehensiveness and perfection, is the sultan of the world of acts.

AL-KARIM

The exceedingly generous and bountiful One who bestows His bounties even upon those who deny His existence. The ability to READ (*iqra*) is only possible through the activation of this Name, which lies dormant within the essence of every individual.

AR-RAQIB

The One who watches over and keeps under control the manifestations of His Names, with His names, at all times.

AL-MUJIB

The One who unequivocally responds to all who turn towards Him (in prayer and invocation) and provides their needs.

AL-WASI

The All-embracing. The One who embraces the whole of existence with the expressions of His Names.

AL-HAKIM

The One whose power of knowledge appears under the guise of 'causes', hence creating causality and leading to the perception of multiplicity.

AL-WADUD

The creator of attraction. The creator of unconditional and unrequited love. The essence within every beloved!

AL-MAJEED

The One whose majestic glory is evident through His magnificent manifestations!

AL-BAITH

The One who constantly transforms new dimensions of existence. As a requisite of the mechanism denoted by the verse **"The One who manifests Himself every moment in yet another wondrous way[27]"**, *al-Baith* continually creates new experiences.

The expression of this name in respect to humanity is depicted in '*amantu*'[28] as 'to believe in life (resurrection) after death' (*bath'u badal mawt*) and the verse **"You will surely experience state after state (you will change dimensions and acquire new bodies in accordance with these dimensions)"**.[29]

We said *ba'th* (resurrection) is to **taste** death and to commence a new state of life after death... However, resurrection is also possible here on earth in this plane of existence. Like the resurrections of *wilayah* (sainthood), *nubuwwah* (prophethood), and *risalah* (the personification of Allah's knowledge)! As all of these stations comprise new states of life.

To give an example, we may say *ba'th* is like the germination of a seed to sprout its plant, or 'give shoot to new life'. Similarly, life emerges from **death** (dormant inactive potential). In relation to the new state of existence, the previous state is considered as a 'grave' (*qabir*).

"And [that they may know] that the Hour (death) **is coming - no doubt about it - and that Allah will resurrect** (by forming new bodies with the Names in their essence) **those** (conscious beings) **in the graves** (bodies)." (Quran 22:7)

ASH-SHAHID

The One who witnesses His existence through His own existence. The One who observes the disclosure of His Names and witnesses His manifestations! The enforcer of the reality that there is no other observer but Himself.

---

[27] Quran 55:29

[28] '*Amantu*' comprises the six fundamentals of belief in Islam. It consists of belief in Allah, His angels, His books, His Rasuls, doomsday (life after death) and destiny (*qadar*), that all good and evil are from Allah.

[29] Quran 84:19

AL-HAQQ

The absolute and unequivocal Reality! The source and essence of every function in manifestation!

AL-WAKIL

The One who provides the means for self-actualization. The One who advocates and protects those who place their trust in Him, providing them with the most auspicious outcomes. He who believes in the potential of the name *al-Wakil* in his own essence, will have confirmed his faith in all the Names (all his potentials). The source of the mystery of **vicegerency** lies in this Name!

AL-QAWWI

The One who transforms His power into the enabling potential for the manifestation of existence (hence comprising the force of the whole of existence).

The One who forms the angelic state.

AL-MATIN

The One who sustains the world of acts, the steadfast, the creator of robustness and stability, the provider of strength and resistance!

AL-WALIYY

The One who guides and enables an individual to discover their reality and to live their life in accordance to their essence. It is the source of *risalah* (personification of Allah's knowledge) and *nubuwwah* (prophethood), which comprise the pinnacle states of sainthood (*wilayah*). It is the dispatcher of the perfected qualities comprising the highest point of sainthood, *risalah*, and the state one beneath that, *nubuwwah*. While the expression of *nubuwwah* is indefinitely functional, the expression of *nubuwwah* applies only to earthly life. A *Nabi* continues to live at the same state of perfection after death, but his explicit role as a *Nabi* is no longer active. On the other hand, due to its inherent saintly qualities, *risalah* continues infinitely (as it does with saints).

AL-HAMID

The One who observes and evaluates His universal perfection on worldly forms manifested by His Name *al-Waliyy*.

Hamd belongs only to Him.

AL-MUHSI

The creator of the 'forms' (micro to macro) comprising the seeming multiplicities, each equipped with unique qualities and attributes, within UNITY.

AL-MUBDI

The One who originates the whole of creation in the corporeal worlds, all with exclusive and unique qualities.

AL-MU'ID

The One who restores life to those who turn back to their essence.

AL-MUHYI

The One who enlivens and enlightens! The One who enables the continuation of the individual's life through the application of knowledge and the observation of one's essential reality.

AL-MUMIT

The One who enables a 'taste' (experience) of death. The One who allows a transition between one state of existence to another.

AL-HAYY

The source of names! The One who gives life to the Names and manifests them. The source of universal energy, the essence of energy!

AL-QAYYUM

The One who renders Himself existent with His own attributes, without the need of anything. Everything in existence subsists with *al-Qayyum*.

AL-WAJID

The One whose qualities and attributes are unfailingly abundant. The manifest One. The One, from which nothing lessens, despite the abundance of His manifestations.

AL-MAJID

The magnificent and glorious One with unrestricted, infinite generosity and endowment (benevolence).

AL-WAHID

The One and only! 'ONE'ness far beyond any concept of multiplicity. The ONE, that isn't composed of (or can be broken into) parts (as in pantheism). The 'ONE'ness that renders duality obsolete! The 'ONE'ness that no mind or intellect can fully comprehend!

AS-SAMAD

The Pure Whole One! Free from the concept of multiplicity! Not formed of adjoining parts. Far from conceptualization and limitation. The self-sufficient One, in need of nothing!

An authentic hadith narrates: "*As-Samad* **is such that it bears no space or emptiness within it** (all, whole, one)."

AL-QADIR

The One who creates (discloses, manifests) and observes His knowledge with His power without depending on causality. The One who is absolutely boundless!

AL-MUQTADIR

The Determiner. The absolute possessor of all power pertaining to creation, governance, and disposition.

AL-MUQADDIM

The One who expedites (or prioritizes) the manifestation of Names according to their purpose of creation.

AL-MU'AKHKHIR

The One who delays manifestation in consonance with His name *al-Hakim*.

AL-AWWAL

The first and initial state of existence, the essential Name.

AL-AKHIR

The infinitely subsequent One, to all creation.

AZ-ZAHIR

The self-evident One, the explicit, unequivocal and perceivable manifestation.

AL-BATIN

The unperceivable reality within the perceivable manifestation! The source of the unknown (*Awwal, Akhir, Zahir, Batin, HU!*)

AL-WALI

The One who governs according to His own verdict.

AL- MUTA'ALI

The limitless, boundless Supreme One, whose supremacy encompasses everything! The One whose reality can never be duly reflected by any engendered, conceptualized existence. The One who is beyond being limited by any mind or intellect.

AL-BARR

The One who eases the actualization of individual temperaments and natural dispositions.

AT-TAWWAB

The One who guides individuals to their essence by enabling them to perceive and comprehend the Reality. The One who allows individuals to repent, that is, to abandon their misdoings and to compensate for any harm that may have been caused. The activation of this Name triggers the name *Rahim*, and thus benevolence and beauty is experienced.

AL-MUNTAQIM

The One who makes individuals live the consequences of their actions that impede in the realization of their essence. To 'avenge' (*zuntiqam*) is to make one 'pay the price' i.e. face the consequence of their doings without exception or pity. Allah is beyond being bound by concepts such as revenge. When used in conjunction with 'severe in retribution' (*shadid'ul iqab*[30]), al-Muntaqim denotes the force that most severely avenges individuals for failing to recognize their essence, by making them live out the consequences of their own obstructive actions in a most severe and intense way.

AL-AFUW

The One who forgives all offences except for 'duality' (*shirq*); the failure to recognize the reality of non-duality prevents the activation of the name *al-Afuw*. Note that to forgive an offence does not mean to compensate the losses of the past, for in the system of *Sunnatullah* there is no compensation of the past!

AR-RA'UF

The compassionate and pitying One who protects individuals who turn to Him from all kinds of behavior which may cause harm or trouble to them.

AL-MAALIK'UL-MULK

The One who governs His Sovereignty as He wishes without having to give account to any individual.

"Say; O Allah, Owner of Sovereignty, You give sovereignty to whom You will and You take sovereignty away from whom You will. You honor whom You will and You humble whom You will. All that is good is in Your hands. Indeed, You are *Qadir* (All-Powerful) over all things." (Quran 3:26)

---

[30] Quran 59:4

DHUL-JALALI WAL-IKRAM

The One who makes individuals experience their 'nothingness' by enabling them to comprehend the reality that they were created from 'naught' and then bestowing them 'Eternity' by allowing them to observe the manifestations of the Names comprising their essence.

AL-MUQSIT

The One who applies justice, as the requirement of His *Uluhiyya*, by endowing every individual their due, based on their unique creation purpose.

AL-JAMI

The One who observes the whole of existence as a multi-dimensional single frame in His Knowledge. The One who gathers creation according to the purpose and function of their creation.

AL-GHANI

The One who is beyond being labeled and limited by the manifestations of His Names, as He is Great (*Akbar*) and beyond all concepts. The One who is infinitely abundant with His Names.

AL-MUGHNI

The One who enriches individuals and raises them above others in wealth and emancipates them. The One who enriches with His own riches. The One who grants the beauty of infinity (*baqa*) which results from '*fakr*' (nothingness).

"Did we not find you poor (*faqr*, in nothingness) and made you rich (with infinity - *baqa*) i.e. Did we not make you a servant of *al-Ghani*? Did we not enrich and emancipate you?)." (Quran 93:8)

"And that it is HU (He) who enriches and deprives." (Quran 53:48)

AL-MANI

The One who prevents those from attaining things they do not deserve!

AD-DARR

The One who afflicts individuals with various distressing situations (sickness, suffering, trouble) in order to make them turn to Himself!

AN-NAFI

The One who prompts individuals to engage in good thoughts and actions to aid them towards beneficent and auspicious outcomes.

AN-NUR

The Knowledge that is the source and essence of everything! The essence of everything is *Nur*; everything is comprised of knowledge. Life subsists with knowledge. Those with knowledge are the ever-living ones (*Hayy*), while those who lack knowledge are like living dead.

AL-HADI

The guide to the truth. The One who allows individuals to live according to their reality. The articulator of the truth. The guide to reality.

AL-BADEE

The incomparable beauty and the originator of beautiful manifestation! The One who originates innumerable manifestations, all with unique and exclusive qualities, and without any example, pattern, specimen etc.

AL-BAQI

The Everlasting. The One who exists beyond the concept of time.

AL-WARITH

The One who manifests under various names and forms in order to inherit and protect the possessions of those who abandon all their belongings to undergo true transformation. When one form is exhausted, He continues His existence with another form.

AR-RASHID

The guider to the right path. The One who allows individuals, who recognize their essential reality, to experience the maturity of this recognition!

AS-SABUR

"And if Allah were to hold responsible the people for their wrongdoings and enforce the consequences upon them at once, He would not have left upon the earth any creature (*DABBAH,*** i.e. earthling, in human 'form' – not human), but He defers them for a specified term. And when their term comes, they can neither remain an hour behind, nor precede it."** (Quran 16:61)

The One who waits for each individual to execute his creation program before rendering effective the consequences of their actions. Allowing the tyranny of the tyrant to take place, i.e. activating the Name *as-Sabur*, is so that both the oppressor and the oppressed can duly carry out their functions before facing the consequences in full effect. Greater calamity forces the creation of increased cruelty.

A FINAL REMINDER

Obviously the meanings of the Names of Allah cannot be confined to such a narrow scope. This is why I refrained from going into this topic for many years. For I know it is impossible to duly cover the comprehensiveness of this topic. However, my own experience of the reflections of this knowledge has compelled me to cover this topic to some extent. I ask Allah's forgiveness. Many books have been written in this field. I only touched upon it based on my understanding today and in a way that is easy to remember. Perhaps I have unveiled only the tip of the iceberg!

SubhanAllahu amma yasifun![31]

I feel I need to reiterate the importance of the following point before concluding this topic:

Everything that I have shared with you here must be observed and experienced within one's consciousness, after becoming cleansed from the restraints of the illusory identity ('I'ness) and the density of the bodily state of existence. **If this cleansing involves the automated repetitions of certain words and phrases without experiential confirmation, the results will be no different from a computer running a program, and hence, ineffective.** Sufism is a way of life! Those who narrate and repeat the words of others (hence gossip!) squander their lives, finding solace in Satan's adorned and embellished games!

The evidence of having attained the reality of this knowledge is the end of suffering! That is, if you are no longer bothered or troubled by anything or anyone, if no situation or person can upset you anymore, it means this knowledge has become your reality! **As long as one is bound by value judgments attached to conditionings and lives his life centered around emotions and behaviors resulting from these, his life will continue and mature as an 'earthling' (not a human) and be subject to 'causality', both here and in the afterlife.**

---

[31] Quran 23:91

Knowledge is for application. So, let us begin with the application of: 'knowledge that is not applied is a weight on one's shoulders!'

Let us ask ourselves at the end of each day:

"Am I ready to embark on a 'one-way' journey tonight in my sleep?"

"Are worldly matters still bothering me and causing me to suffer? Or am I living my servitude in peace and happiness?"

If your answer is 'Yes', glad tidings to you my friend! If it is 'No', then many tasks await you tomorrow! In this case, when you wake up in the morning, ask yourself "What must I do today in order to go to bed in total peace and happiness tonight?"

Glory be to the One who allows us to live our days with the awareness that everything we own will perish...

Wassalam...

A special thank you to the honorable imam of Istanbul Kanlica Mosque, Hasan Guler Hodja, a venerable scholar and an exemplary man of knowledge, for sharing his valuable insight with me and for assisting me with *'Decoding The Quran'*.

AHMED HULUSI
03 February 2009
North Carolina, USA

6

SELECTED VERSES FROM THE BOOK OF
ALLAH

1. "'O you who have believed; *Aminu B'illahi*[32]**' That is, 'O you who have believed, believe in Allah in accord with the meaning signified by the letter B.'..."** (Quran 4:136)

2. "And of the people are some who say, 'We believe in Allah (in accord with the meaning of the letter B – that His Names comprise our being) **and the life after'** (that we will forever live the consequences of our deeds), **but they are not believers** (in accord with the meaning of the letter B)." (Quran 2:8)

3. "So believe in Allah, whose Names comprise the essence of your being, and his Rasul, the Ummi Nabi, who believes in Allah, the essence of his self, and what He disclosed..." (Quran 7:158)

4. "As for those who believe in Allah, the essence of everything, and hold fast unto Him as their essential reality –

---

[32] What does this mean? It means: Among all the worlds that are constituted by the meanings of the Names of Allah, your reality, existence and being also comprise the Names of Allah. Your Rabb, your very Reality is the al-Asma (the Names). Therefore, neither you nor anything else around you is anything other than the manifestations of these Names. So do not be of those who fail to see this non-dual reality, and who give a separate existence to things (like God) they believe is 'other' than Allah. Such duality will only result in burning, both in this life and the next. For further information: *Introductory Information to Understanding the Quran*

HU will admit them to grace (*rahmah*) **and bounty** (the awareness of the qualities of the Names) **and guide them to Himself** (enable the observation of their innermost essence) **on a straight path** (*sirat al-mustaqim*)." (Quran 4:175)

5. **"And when it is said to them, 'Believe what Allah has revealed** (the knowledge that the Names of Allah comprise the entire existence, your very being and the knowledge of *sunnatullah*),' **they say, 'No, rather, we will follow that which we found our fathers following** (external deification).' **What if their fathers were misguided and failed to understand the reality?"** (Quran 2:170)

6. **"...Verily Allah is *Ghani* from the worlds** (in terms of His Absolute Essence, Allah is free from being conditioned and limited by the manifested compositions of His Names)." (Quran 29:06)

7. **"...There is nothing that resembles HU!..."** (Quran 42:11)

8. **"Every constructed sense of self** (ego) **on the earth** (corporeal life) **is illusory** (inexistent). ***Al-Baqi*** (eternal, without being subject to the concept of time) **is the face** (absolute reality) **of your *Rabb*** (the meanings of the Names comprising your essence), **the *Dhul-Jalali Wal-Ikram*."** (Quran 55:26-27)

9. **"Sensory perception perceives Him not but He perceives** (evaluates) **all perception..."** (Quran 6:103)

10. **"...Never can '*You*'** (with your illusory self – ego) **see** (comprehend) **'*Me*'...** (Absolute Reality, Absolute 'I')..." (Quran 7:143)

11. **"They did not justly appraise** (the manifestations of the qualities denoted by the name) **Allah ..."** (Quran 22:74)

12. **"*Rahman* is established on the Throne"** (*Rahman* established His sovereignty by creating the worlds [the existential world created by the potential of the Names inherent in one's brain] with His Names, i.e. *Rahman* observes His knowledge with His knowledge, in the quantum potential)." (Quran 20:5)

13. **"Verily, when He wills a thing, His Command is, '*Kun* = be'** (He merely wishes it to be), **and it is** (formed with ease)! ***Subhan* is He in whose hand** (governance) **is the *Malakut*** (the

force of the Names) **of all things, and to Him you will be returned** (the illusory self – ego will come to an end and the Absolute Reality will be discerned)." (Quran 36:82-83)

14. "Within your own selves (the essence of the self). **Will you still not see** (discern)?" (Quran 51:21)

15. "And whoever is blind (unable to perceive the truth) **in this life** (outer life) **will also be blind in the eternal life to come** (inner life) **and further astray in way** (of thought)." (Quran 17:72)

16. "HU is the *Al-Awwal* (the first and initial state of existence) **and *Al-Akhir*** (the infinitely subsequent One, to all manifestation), *Az-Zahir* (the explicit, unequivocal and perceivable manifestation; the Absolute Reality beyond the illusion) **and *Al-Batin...*** (the unperceivable reality within the perceivable manifestation, the source of the unknown; the Absolute Self beyond the illusory selves) (There is nothing other than HU)." (Quran 57:3)

17. "...We are closer to him than his jugular vein (within the dimensions of the brain)!" (Quran 50:16)

18. "...And He is with you (the origin of your being) **wherever you are** (as your reality exists with His Names)... (This points to the unity of existence beyond the illusion of duality)." (Quran 57:4)

19. "...So wherever you turn, there is the face of Allah (you are face to face with the manifestation of the qualities denoted by Allah's Names)..." (Quran 2:115)

20. "...Be careful! Verily He is *Al-Muhit* (the One who forms the existence of all things with the qualities of His Names)." (Quran 41:54)

21. "...Fear me (for you will face the consequences of your deeds based on the mechanics of the system; *sunnatullah*), **if you are of the believers."** (Quran 3:175)

22. "...Which will tell them that man had *no certainty* in Our signs (they were unable to observe the qualities of the names that comprise their being)." (Quran 27:82)

23. "...Verily, if you follow their desires (ideas and wants formed by their conditionings) **after what has come to you of**

knowledge be among the wrongdoers (those who punish themselves as a result of their failure to discern their essential reality)." (Quran 2:145)

24. "Set your face (consciousness) **as a *Hanif*** (without the concept of a deity-god, without making *shirq* to Allah, i.e. with the consciousness of non-duality) **towards the One Religion** (the only system and order)**, the natural disposition** (*fitrah*) **of Allah** (i.e. the primary system and mechanism of the brain) **upon which Allah has created man. There is no change in the creation of Allah. This is the infinitely valid System** (*deen al-qayyim*) **but most people do not know."** (Quran 30:30)

25. "And We have created the heavens (the stages of manifestation pertaining to the qualities denoted by the Names) **and earth** (man's illusory world) **and everything in between them in Absolute Truth."** (Quran 15:85)

26. "... Say: 'Allah' and let them amuse themselves in their empty discourse (their illusory world) **in which they're absorbed."** (Quran 6:91)

27. "...And you threw not, when you (illusory self; ego) **threw, but it was Allah who threw..."** (Quran 8:17)

28. "He is not questioned for what He does! (as there is no duality!)**..."** (Quran 21:23)

29. "...He creates whatever He wills..." (Quran 42:49)

30. "...Indeed, Allah does as He wills (He forms what He wills to manifest from His knowledge with Power; Knowledge – Will – Power)**."** (Quran 22:14)

31. "...Allah does as He wills (Allah manifests the qualities of His Names that He wishes!)**."** (Quran 14:27)

32. "...Allah enables the observation of his innermost essential reality to whom He wills." (Quran 22:16)

33. "...Allah (the Names [the various compositions of structural qualities constituting existence] within the essence of man) **enables the realization of His *Nur*** (the knowledge of the Absolute Reality beyond what is perceived) **whom He wills."** (Quran 24:35)

34. "**Whoever Allah enables the observation of his innermost essential essence, he is the one who reaches the reality...**" (Quran 7:178)

35. "**He who Allah enables the observation of his innermost essential reality can never be led astray!...**" (Quran 39:37)

36. "**...Allah enables those who turn to Him to realize their inner reality!**" (Quran 42:13)

37. "**He gives wisdom** (the system by which the qualities of the Names are manifested) **to whom He wills, and whoever has been given wisdom has certainly been given much benefit. And none will discern this except those with intellect and deep contemplative skills.**" (Quran 2:269)

38. "**Allah chooses** (enables the comprehension of one's inner reality) **for Himself whom He wills...**" (Quran 42:3)

39. "**...Such is the bounty of Allah** (the realization of the vastness of the qualities of the Names), **which He grants unto whomever He wills...**" (Quran 57:21)

40. "**And whomsoever Allah wills the realization of his essential reality, He opens his breast** (his innermost comprehension) **to Islam** (to the consciousness of his submission) **and whomsoever He wills to lead astray, He makes his breast tight and constricted, as though he were laboriously climbing into the sky!...**" (Quran 6:125)

41. "**...but Allah purifies** (from the illusory self; ego) **whom He wills...**" (Quran 24:21)

42. "**He who purifies** (his consciousness) **has succeeded.**" (Quran 91:9)

43. "**...Know well, that** (if you do not attend to this invitation) **Allah will intervene between the person's consciousness and his heart** (Allah creates a barrier between his emotions and reason, abandoning him to an emotional state of existence that comprises his hell through the system of the brain) **and prevent him. To Him you will be resurrected** (you will reside in a realm in which the Absolute Reality will become apparent; you will be evaluated by the qualities of the names that comprise your essence)." (Quran 8:24)

44. "**...Every instance HU** (the Absolute Essence of Existence) **manifests Himself in yet another way.**" (Quran 55:29)

45. "**Allah abolishes what He wills or forms** (into a perceivable reality, what He wills)**, and with Him is the Mother of the Book** (primary knowledge; the knowledge of the ways in which the Names will manifest at every instant)." (Quran 13:39)

46. "**My decision** (rule) **will not be altered!...**" (Quran 50:29)

47. "**...And Allah gives provision** (both limited sustenance for the corporeal life and infinite life sustenance pertaining to the realization of one's inner reality and its benefits) **to whom He wills without account.**" (Quran 2:212)

48. "**...To each of you We prescribed a law** (rules and conditions regarding lifestyle) **and a method** (a system based on fixed realities not subject to change within time)**...**" (Quran 5:48)

49. "**The Rasul** (Muhammad (saw)) **has believed in what was revealed** (knowledge that emerged from the dimensional depths) **to him** (to his consciousness) **from his *Rabb*** (the qualities of the Names of Allah comprising his essential reality)." (Quran 2:285)

50. "**...We make no distinction between** (the ways in which the knowledge of Allah was revealed to) **His Rasuls...**" (Quran 2:285)

51. "**...Had Allah willed, He would surely have enabled the realization of the absolute reality to all of mankind...**" (Quran 13:31)

52. "**And if We had willed, We could have enabled every being** (illusory self; ego) **to realize its essential reality, but My word: 'I will surely fill Hell** (the conditions to manifest the specific configuration of the qualities of the Names that result in an infernal state of life) **with *jinn* and man all together' is in effect.**" (Quran 32:13)

53. "**Had your *Rabb*** (the reality of the Names comprising your essence) **willed, all those who live on earth would surely have had faith** (in the qualities of the Names of Allah that comprise his being and all that is manifested through him)**, all of them entirely... So then, will you compel the people to become believers? And it is**

not for a soul to believe unless the unique composition of Allah's Names comprising his essence permits." (Quran 10:99-100)

54. "No more is the Rasul bound to do except to provide the knowledge (of the reality and its requisites)..." (Quran 5:99)

55. "There is no compulsion in [acceptance of] the religion (the system and order of Allah; *sunnatullah*)..." (Quran 2:256)

56. "...and never will suffering occur unless a Rasul of the absolute reality is revealed." (Quran 17:15)

57. "And We have not revealed you except as grace to the worlds (people)." (Quran 21: 107)

58. "...but [he is] the Rasul of Allah, the final of Nabis (the summit of perfection)." (Quran 33:40)

59. "O covered one; arise and awaken!" (Quran 74:1-2)

60. "Say (O Rasul): 'I am only a man like you (aside from the knowledge of Allah disclosed through me [*Risalat*], we possess the same reality).'" (Quran 18:110)

61. "And obey Allah and His Rasul..." (Quran 8:46)

62. "Indeed, the religion (system and order) in the sight of Allah is Islam (the whole of creation is in a state of submission, whether conscious or unconscious of the qualities of the Names)..." (Quran 3:19)

63. "And whoever seeks a religion (system and order) other than Islam (the consciousness of being in a state of submission) his search will be ineffective! ..." (Quran 3:85)

64. "Whose heart (essence) Allah has expanded towards comprehending Islam, is he not upon a *Nur* (knowledge) disclosed by his *Rabb* (his essential reality)? ..." (Quran 39:22)

65. "This day I have perfected for you your religion (your acquisition of religious knowledge) and completed My favor upon you and have approved for you Islam (complete submission to Allah) as (the understanding of) religion..." (Quran 5:3)

66. **"It is HU who shapes** (forms, programs) **you in the womb** (mother's womb – in Arabic *rahim*; the productive mechanism within your essence: *rahimiyyah*) **as He wishes..."** (Quran 3:6)

67. **"...But if good comes to them, they say, 'This is from Allah'; and if evil befalls them, they say, 'This is from you.' Say, 'All** [things] **are from Allah...'"** (Quran 4:78)

68. **"Your *Rabb*** (reality of the Names comprising your essence) **creates and chooses as He pleases, they have no free will** (or choice)**..."** (Quran 28:68)

69. **"Who brings the living** (the consciousness of being alive with the Names of the *Hayy*) **out of the dead** (the futile state of corporeal existence) **and brings the dead** (the state of being blinded to the reality of one's self or the reality of others; confining one's existence only to the body and assuming life is going to end once the body deteriorates under the soil) **out of the living** (while in respect of his essential reality he is alive)**? Who carries out the judgment? They will say, 'Allah'..."** (Quran 10:31)

70. **"...And whoever is grateful, his gratitude is for his self** (the realization and evaluation of the perfection of his essence)**..."** (Quran 27:40)

71. **"When a** [single] **disaster struck you, although we had struck** [the enemy] **with one twice as great, you said, 'Why and how did this come about?' Say, 'It has come about from yourselves** (your ego)**'. Indeed, Allah is *Qadir*** (the possessor of continual and infinite power) **over all things."** (Quran 3:165)

72. **"...He who submits to, and places his trust in Allah, Allah will be sufficient for him** (he who believes in the forces pertaining to the qualities of the Names comprising his essence and complies with their requirements, those forces will be ever sufficient for him)**."** (Quran 65:3)

73. **"...Seek the continual manifestation of the Names of Allah** (from your essence in respect of its *Uluhiyyah*; from the forces of the Names comprising your being) **and have patience..."** (Quran 7:128)

74. "And your *Rabb* has decreed that you serve only Him (He created you to manifest the qualities of His Names)..." (Quran 17:23)

75. "I have created the *jinn* and men only so that they may serve Me (by means of manifesting the qualities of My Names)." (Quran 51:56)

76. "He is *al-Badee* (The originator of the heavens [states of consciousness] and the earth [the body] who makes things without any sample or like). When He wills a thing, He only says to it, 'Be,' and it is." (Quran 2:117)

77. "...While it is Allah who created you and all your doings." (Quran 37:96)

78. "Do you not see that to Allah prostrates whoever is in the heavens and whoever is on the earth, the sun, the moon, the stars, the mountains, the trees, the moving creatures and many of the people? But upon many the suffering has been justified. And he whom Allah humiliates – for him there is no bestower of honor. Indeed, Allah does what He wills." (Quran 22:18)

79. "Say: 'Everyone acts according to his own creation program (natural disposition; *fitrah*).'..." (Quran 17:84)

80. "And to Him belongs whoever is in the heavens (conscious beings) and the earth (bodily beings). Thus, all are in a state of devout obedience to Him (in manifesting the qualities of His Names)..." (Quran 30:26)

81. "...The seven heavens (all creation within the seven dimensions of consciousness) and the earth (the bodies) and whatever is in them *continue their existence through* Him (*tasbih*). And there is not a thing that does not continue its existence through His *hamd* (the reality of the Names comprising one's essence [*Rabb*] is the evaluator of this continual existence), but you do not understand their [way of, discourse, disposition] disclosure..." (Quran 17:44)

82. "...There is no animate creature but that He holds its forehead (the brain; the very qualities of the Names of Allah!)..." (Quran 11:56)

83. **"You cannot will unless Allah wills** (your will is Allah's will)..." (Quran 76:30)

84. **"Indeed we have created everything with its program** (*qadar*)." (Quran 54:49)

85. **"And there is not a thing of which its depositories** (the forces comprising it) **is not with us! And We disclose** (the forces/qualities) **according to its program. The requirements of its core creation program unfold sequentially."** (Quran 15:21)

86. **"No calamity befalls you on earth** (on your physical body and outer world) **or among yourselves** (your inner world) **that has not already been recorded in a book** (formed in the dimension of knowledge) **before We bring it into being! Indeed for Allah, this is easy. We inform you of this in order that you don't despair over your losses or exult** (in pride) **over what We have given you, for Allah does not like the boastful and the arrogant!"** (Quran 57:22-23)

87. **"...Perhaps you hate a thing and it is good for you; and perhaps you love a thing and it is bad for you. And Allah knows, while you know not."** (Quran 2:216)

88. **"Whatever good comes to you it is from Allah, but whatever evil comes to you it is from your self** (from complying with your conditioned beliefs including your alleged 'moral codes')..." (Quran 4:79)

89. **"...Indeed, the *dhikr*** (remembrance) **of Allah is Akbar** (enables one to experience *Akbariyyah* – Absolute Magnificence)..." (Quran 29:45)

90. **"...and engage much in the *dhikr*** (contemplation on the forces of the Names comprising your essence) **of Allah so you can overcome difficulties and attain salvation."** (Quran 8:45)

91. **"...And remember** (*dhikr*) **Him, to the extent of your awareness of your innermost essential reality..."** (Quran 2:198)

92. **"Allah will never hold anyone responsible for that which they have no capacity..."** (Quran 2:286)

93. "Remember (*dhikr*) the qualities of the Names comprising your essence; your *Rabb*, and seclude yourself to Him in complete devotion." (Quran 73:8)

94. "So remember (*dhikr*) Me; so that I will remember you." (Quran 2:152)

95. "...And remember Allah while standing, sitting, or [lying] on your sides** (i.e. experience Him in your being at all times)...**" (Quran 4:103)

96. "**They** (those who have attained the essence of the reality) **remember Allah while standing or sitting or [lying] on their sides...**" (Quran 3:191)

97. "**And if you speak your thoughts** (or conceal them,) **know that indeed He knows the secret** (in your consciousness) **and what is [even] deeper** (the actual Names that compose it)**.**" (Quran 20:7)

98. "**O believers! Let not your worldly goods or your children prevent you from the remembrance of Allah** (the remembrance of your essential self and the resulting experience)**. And whoever does this – it is they who are the losers!**" (Quran 63:9)

99. "**And he who turns away from My *dhikr*** (the absolute reality of which I have reminded him) **indeed, he will have a restricted life** (limited by the conditions of his body and mind)**, and We will resurrect him as blind on the day** (period) **of resurrection.**" (Quran 20:124)

100. "**They** (the objects/idols of their worship) **will say, '*Subhan*, You are! It is not possible for us to take besides You any allies. But when You provided comforts for them and their fathers, they forgot the knowledge of reality and indulged in bodily pleasures eventually leading to their ruin.**'" (Quran 25:18)

101. "...**And whoever is blinded** (with external things) **from the remembrance of *Rahman*** (remembering that his essential reality is composed of the Names of Allah and thus from living the requirements of this) **We appoint for him a Satan** (a delusion; the idea that he is only the physical body and that life should be lived in pursuit of bodily pleasures) **and this** (belief) **will become his** (new) **identity! And indeed, these will avert them from the way** [the

path to reality] **while they think that they are on the right path."**
(Quran 43:36-37)

102. "Satan (corporeality; the idea of being just the physical
body) **has overcome them and made them forget the
remembrance of Allah** (their own reality of which they have been
reminded, and that they will abandon their bodies and live for
eternity as 'consciousness' comprised of Allah's names!) **Those are
the acquaintances of Satan** (those who are receptive to satanic
impulses and who think of themselves as only the physical body).
**Beware, for most assuredly, the party of Satan will be the very
losers!"** (Quran 58:19)

**103. "[Are] men whom neither trade nor worldly dealings
distracts from the *dhikr* of Allah** (remembering their essential
reality) **and performance of *salat*** (experiencing their essence) **and
giving of *zakah*** (unrequited sharing)." (Quran 24:37)

**104. "And when My servants ask you concerning Me – indeed
I am Qarib** (so close that you are naught; only I exist... Let us
remember the verse 'I am nearer than the jugular vein'). **I respond
to the one who turns to me and asks of Me** (in prayer)..." (Quran
2:186)

105. "...And never will you find in the System (course) **of Allah**
(*sunnatullah*) **any change."** (Quran 48:23)

106. "...You will never see a change in *sunnatullah* (the
mechanics of Allah's system)." (Quran 35:43)

107. "Maintain *salat* (prayer; turning to Allah) **with care** [in
particular] **the middle *salat*** (*asr* prayer – the constant experience of
this reality in one's consciousness)..." (Quran 2:238)

108. "So woe to those who pray (due to tradition), **who are
heedless** (cocooned) **of** (the experience of the meaning of) **their
*salat*** (which is an ascension [*miraj*] to their innermost essential
reality; their *Rabb*)." (Quran 107:4-5)

109. "They (the believers) **are awed by the experience of
observing the qualities of Allah's Names."** (Quran 23:2)

110. "...Among His servants, only those who have knowledge
(of what is denoted by the name Allah and who are aware of its

Might) **truly feel awe towards Allah!** (realize their nothingness in respect of His magnificence)..." (Quran 35:28)

111. "Certainly, I have turned my face (my consciousness), **cleansed from the concept of a deity** (*Hanif*), **toward '*Al-Fatir*'** (He who creates everything programmed according to its purpose) **who created the heavens and the earth, and I am not of the dualists."** (Quran 6:79)

112. "Did you not see the one who had deified his '*hawa*' (instinctual desires, bodily form, illusionary self)..!" (Quran 25:43)

113. "Indeed, Allah does not forgive (apparent or discrete forms of) *shirq* (i.e. directly or indirectly assuming the existence of beings 'other' than Allah, whether external objects [apparent] or our own egos [discrete]; thereby fragmenting the non-dual reality), **but He forgives lesser sins other than this** (*ma doona*) ('lesser sins' here connotes the perception that actions are initiated by the self/ego rather than by Allah), **as He wills..."** (Quran 4:48)

114. "...Certainly, if you live in a state of duality (*shirq*), **all your doings would surely become worthless and you would surely become among the losers..."** (Quran 39:65)

115. "We will cast fear into the hearts of those who deify their egos (duality) **over the Names of Allah comprising their essence, and cover the absolute reality within, even though there is no evidence that their ego-identities actually exist! And their abode will be the fire..."** (Quran 3:151)

116. "...Assuredly, duality is a great injustice/wrongdoing (duality, which denotes the denial of one's essential qualities referenced as the Names of Allah, leads to one's deprivation from these core qualities)." (Quran 31:13)

117. "Verily the dualists (who claim the existence of their ego-identities alongside the Absolute Oneness) **are contaminated..."** (Quran 9:28)

118. "...None but the purified (from the dirt of *shirq* – duality – animalistic nature) **can touch it** (i.e. become enlightened with the Knowledge of the Absolute Reality)." (Quran 56:79)

119. "**Do not assume the existence of a god** (exterior manifestations of power or your illusory self) **besides Allah. For there is no God. Only HU! Everything** (in respect of its thingness) **is inexistent, only the face of HU** (only that which pertains to the Absolute Reality) **exists!...**" (Quran 28:88)

120. "**Do not make** [up in your mind] **another deity besides Allah** (do not deify your illusory selves)! **Lest you find yourself disgraced and forsaken** (as a result of your *shirq*, dualistic understanding, you will be confined to the limits of your ego rather than manifesting the infinite potential of your essence)." (Quran 17:22)

121. "**Allah knows with certainty that none exists other than He. He is HU, there is no other, only HU... and** (so do) **the forces** (potentials) **of His names** (angels; compositions of qualities that manifest through the knowledge of reality) **and those of knowledge** (those who possess this knowledge also know, and thus testify this reality) **and maintain themselves in accord with this truth...**" (Quran 3:18)

122. "**Had there been within both** (the heavens [meanings] and the earth [actions]) **gods besides Allah, verily this system would have lost its order. So exalted** (*subhan*) **is Allah, *Rabb* of the Throne** (who creates and forms existence from the quantum potential, at will) **beyond the definitions they attribute to Him.**" (Quran 21:22)

123. "**So magnificent is He Who forms constellations in the skies** (the materialization of the various compositional groups of His Names at the macro level)**...**" (Quran 25:61)

124. "**Indeed, We have adorned earth's heaven** (configured man's brain) **with planets** (astrological data) **and protected it from every rebellious Satan** (the purified consciousness is beyond the reach of illusory impulses)." (Quran 37:6-7)

125. "**...And the stars are subjected by and in service to His command** (the stars are also a manifestation of the meanings of the Names comprising their essence)**...**" (Quran 16:12)

126. "**He governs the earth** (the brain) **from the heaven** (through the cosmic electromagnetic energy emanating from the qualities of the Names in the form of celestial constellations [star signs] that affect the second brain in the gut and thus one's consciousness, or from an internal perspective, through the Names that become manifest in one's brain based on the holographic reality)..." (Quran 32:5)

127. "Allah is He who has created seven heavens and of the earth, the like of them. [His] command continually manifests among them (astrological [angelic] influences that are also manifestations of Allah's names and their effect on creation)." (This verse should be contemplated upon in depth!) (Quran 65:12)

128. "And indeed it is HU who is the *Rabb* of Sirius (star)!" (Quran 53:49)

129. "And leads to the reality by the (Names comprising the essence of the) **stars** (the people of reality, the hadith: 'My Companions are like the stars; whoever among them you follow, you will reach the truth')...!" (Quran 16:16)

130. "Had there not been a time (*dahr*), **when the name of man was not uttered?** (What is the validity of a piece of ice in the vastness of the ocean? i.e. man was not yet manifest; he was the unmanifest within the dimension of the Names)." (Quran 76:1)

131. "And [mention] when your *Rabb* took from the children of Adam, from their loins (semen, genes), **their descendants and made them testify to themselves, [asking them], 'Am I not your *Rabb*?' and they said, 'Yes, indeed we bear witness!'** [Of this we remind you] – **lest you say on the day of Resurrection, 'We were cocooned** (unaware of this knowledge) **of this'** (This refers to man being created upon the natural disposition of Islam)." (Quran 7:172)

132. "And they (the Rabbis) **ask you, [O Muhammad], about the spirit. Say, 'The spirit is under the command of my *Rabb*** (Amr; the manifestation of the Names). **And you have been given little of this knowledge'** (this answer is for the Rabbis who asked this question)." (Quran 17:85)

133. "I will make upon the earth (the body) **a vicegerent** (conscious beings who will live with the awareness of the Names)." (Quran 2:30)

134. "**And He taught** (manifested and programmed) **Adam all of the Names** (all potential pertaining to the Names)..." (Quran 2:31)

135. "**We have certainly created man in the best of forms** (with the qualities of the Names). **Then We reduced him to the lowest of the low** (to the/their world of conditionings)." (Quran 95:4-5)

136. "**Who created you, formed you** (created you with a program to form your brain, an individual consciousness and a spirit) **and balanced you** (the work process of your brain, consciousness and spirit)! **Whatever form** (manifestation of Names) **He willed for you, He configured your composition accordingly.**" (Quran 82:7-8)

137. "**By the self and the One who formed** (the brain)**, and inspired it** (individual consciousness) (with discernment of) **its wickedness** (its capacity to be misguided from the Reality and the System) **and its righteousness** (protection)." (Quran 91:7-8)

138. "**And serve your *Rabb* until there comes to you the certainty!** (the observation that your identity or ego is an illusion and inexistent, and the only valid reality is the Names; that death is the realization of the absolute reality; the experience of the *Wahid'ul Qahhar*) (after this certainty, servitude to one's *Rabb* will continue as the natural outcome of this process)" (Quran 15:99)

139. "**And man will only accrue the results** (consequences) **of his own labor** (what manifests through him; his thoughts and actions, due to the trigger system)[33]**.**" (Quran 53:39)

140. "**During this period every individual consciousness will be requited for what he has done** (face the consequences of his deeds) **no injustice** [will be done] **in this time: verily, Allah instantly puts into effect the consequences of one's actions.**" (Quran 40:17)

141. "**...And you will not be recompensed except for what you did** (your own actions)**!**" (Quran 36:54)

---

[33] The trigger system

142. **"...And Allah did not cause them to suffer, but it was they** (their constructed self, ego-identity) **who caused their own suffering."** (Quran 29:40)

143. **"And there are ranks based on what they manifest, so they may be fully compensated for their deeds, without any injustice."** (Quran 46:19)

144. **"Indeed, you will be tasters of the painful suffering. And you will not be recompensed except for what you did** (your own actions)." (Quran 37:38-39)

145. **"This is the result of what your hands have put forth. Verily, Allah is never unjust to [His] servants** (Allah is not the cause of your dual perception; it is the ego or your constructed identity who attributes a separate existence to itself, hence causing duality [*shirq*] which leads to suffering)." (Quran 22:10)

146. **"And this apparent and perceived worldly life** (the lowest state of consciousness) **is no other than an amusement** (a delusive diversion in relation to the real) **and a game** (in which we merely play our roles in the script)!" (Quran 29:64)

147. **"Realize well that the life of this world is but an amusement and diversion and adornment and boasting to one another and competition in increase of wealth and children... The things pertaining to the worldly life are nothing but a delusion."** (Quran 57:20)

148. **"And We will surely test you** (your state of duality, *shirq*) **with fear and hunger and a loss of wealth and lives** (the lives of those who are dear to you) **and the produce of your labor, but give good tidings to the patient** (those who refrain from reacting impulsively and wait to see how things will turn out)." (Quran 2:155)

149. **"Never will you experience the essence of reality** (*albirra*) **until you unrequitedly give away from that which you love most..."** (Quran 3:92)

150. **"...They follow only assumption and the illusory desires of their ego** (even though) **the knowledge of Reality has indeed**

come to them from their *Rabb* (the reality of the Names comprising their essence)." (Quran 53:23)

151. "And they have no proof thereof. They follow only unverifiable assumptions, and indeed, never can assumption reflect the truth." (Quran 53:28)

152. "Your assumption about your *Rabb* has brought you to perdition, and you have become among the losers." (Quran 41:23)

153. "O you who have believed, avoid most assumptions (guesswork about things of which you have no certain knowledge). Indeed, some assumptions are an offence (lead to or are an outcome of duality). And do not spy on others (do not inspect or inquire into the private matters of others out of curiosity) and do not backbite. Would one of you like to eat the flesh of his dead brother? You would detest it! ..." (Quran 49:12)

154. "And for all people a specified term (lifespan) is set. So when the end of their time has come, they can neither delay it by a single moment, nor can they hasten it[34]." (Quran 7:34)

155. "Every individual consciousness will taste death (life without a biological body will continue eternally)..." (Quran 3:185)

156. "And never think of those who have been killed in the cause of Allah as dead. Rather, they are alive with their *Rabb* receiving provision (from the forces pertaining to their innermost essential reality)." (Quran 3:169)

157. "They will not taste death therein except the first death (they will forever)." (Quran 44:56)

158. "During that period (the eternal life) they will see that is as though they had not remained [in the world] except for an '*Ashiyyah*' (the time it takes for the sun to set below the horizon) or the period of twilight." (Quran 79:46)

159. "How can you deny that the Names of Allah comprise your essence (in accord with the letter B)? When you were lifeless (dead; unaware of your essential reality) and He brought you to life

---

[34] The incapacity of the people to discern the Nabi does not render the Nabi ineffective, but rather, suggests the end of the comprehension of that populace.

(with the knowledge He disclosed to you); **again He will cause you to die** (from the state of thinking you are only the body), **and again He will bring you to life** (purify you from confining your existence to your body and enable you to live in a state of consciousness)... **Eventually you will see your reality!**" (Quran 2:28)

160. **"And Allah causes you to grow from the earth gradually like a plant** (the body that comes from the earth continues its life as consciousness). **Then He will return you into it and again extract you from it. And Allah has made for you the earth an exhibition** (living environment), **so that you may traverse therein, on spacious ways."** (Quran 71:17-20)

161. **"So when death finally comes to one of them, he says, 'My *Rabb*, send me back** (to worldly life) **so I may do what is necessary for my eternal future** (i.e. a faithful life which I did not heed or give importance to; the potential that I did not use and activate).' **No!** (It is impossible to go back!) **His words are useless!** (His request is unrecognized in the system) **and behind them is a barrier** (an isthmus, a difference of dimension) **until the Day they are resurrected** (they cannot go back; reincarnation, being re-born for another worldly life is not possible!). **So when the Horn is blown** (when the process of resurrection, i.e. a new beginning, commences), **no relationship** (worldly interactions, family relations, titles or familiar faces) **will there be among them that Day, nor will they ask about one another** (in terms of earthly relations)." (Quran 23:101)

162. **"[It will be] during the period the earth** (the body) **will be replaced by another earth** (another body), **and the heavens as well** (individual consciousness will also be turned into another system of perception)..."** (Quran 14:48)

163. **"They will murmur among themselves, 'You remained** (in the world) **only ten [hours].'"** (Quran 20:103)

164. **"[It will be said], 'You were certainly in unmindfulness of this** (you were living in your cocoon), **and We have removed from you your veil, so your sight, from this period on, is sharp.'"** (Quran 50:22)

165. "READ the knowledge (book) of your life! Sufficient is your self (your consciousness) **against you at this stage as an accountant** (witness the results of your thoughts and actions during your worldly life lest you judge others)." (Quran 17:14)

166. "If you could but see when they are confronted with the fire (suffering) **they will say 'Oh, if only we can go back** (to our biological life on earth; as biological life is required to activate the forces within the brain) **and not deny the signs of our *Rabb*** (our intrinsic divine qualities and potential deriving from the Names that comprise our essential reality) **and be among the believers. But that which they concealed before** (the knowledge of reality with which that had been endowed) **has now become apparent to them. And even if they were returned they would return to the things from which they had been forbidden, they are liars indeed. And they say, 'There is none but our worldly life, and we will not be resurrected, if you could but see when they will be made to stand before their *Rabb*** (when they recognize and become aware of the potentials of the Names within their own reality). **He will say, 'Is this not the Reality?' They will say, 'Yes, it is our *Rabb*.' He will then say, 'So taste the punishment now as the consequence of denying the knowledge of reality."** (Quran 6:27-30)

167. "And that Day (period) **Hell will be brought** (to enclose the earth) **– during this period man will remember and think, but what benefit to him will the remembrance (*dhikr*) be** (when he no longer has a body – brain with which he can develop his spirit)?" **He will say "I wish I had done beneficial things** (raised my consciousness level to observe the Names)." (Quran 89:23-24)

168. "Indeed, Hell has become a place of passage (everyone will pass from it)." (Quran 78:21)

169. "And there is none of you who he will not encounter (experience) **hell. This is, by your *Rabb*, a definite decree. Then We will save those who protected themselves** (who exhibit the forces that become manifest as a result of living ones reality) **and leave the transgressors on their knees!"** (Quran 19:71-72)

170. "When they are shown to each other... To save themselves from the punishment of that period, the guilty ones

will want to offer their sons to the fire in their stead... And his wife and his brother; and his nearest kindred who shelter him and everything on earth so that it could save him!" (Quran 70:11-14)

171. "Indeed we have warned you of a close suffering (caused by the realization of the truth through the experience of death)! On that day, man will observe what his hands have put forth, and those who denied the knowledge of reality will say 'Oh, how I wish I was dust!'" (Quran 78:40)

172. "On that Day the (hypocrite) men and two-faced women will say to those who believed, 'Wait for us that we may acquire some of your light (*nur*; knowledge of reality).' It will be said, 'Go back and seek light.' And a wall will be placed between them with a door, its interior (inner world) containing grace, but its exterior is torment (the condition of those who fail to experience the reality is suffering, whereas observing the qualities of the Names leads to a state of grace)." (Quran 57:13)

173. "[On] the Day (during that period) Allah will not disgrace the Nabi and those who shared his faith. Their light (*nur*) will proceed before them and on their right; they will say, 'Our Rabb, perfect our *nur* (increase the scope of our observation) and forgive us...'" (Quran 66:8)

174. "So Allah conferred favor upon us and protected us from the suffering of the (hellfire; the state of burning) *samum* (an infusing microwave radiation that is harmful to the astral body)!" (Quran 52:27)

175. "In the sight of your *Rabb* (the perception at the level of your essential reality manifested by the forces comprising your being) one day is like one thousand (earthly) years! (Allah knows best but I believe this verse is in reference to the perception pertaining to the dimension of life after death, for, 'your *Rabb*' connotes the state of consciousness [the perception of time in one's brain or cocoon reality] as a result of one's *individual Rabb* or composition of Names. This is not in reference to the '*Rabb* of the worlds')" (Quran 22:47)

176. "**The angels and the Spirit will return to their essence in a period** (which will seem to you to be) **of fifty thousand years** (the period of time to reach Allah in their essence)." (Quran 70:4)

177. "**READ** (grasp) **with the Name of your** *Rabb* (with the knowledge that comprises your being), **who created. Created man from** *alaq* (a clot of blood; genetic composition). **Read! For your** *Rabb* **is** *Akram* (most generous). **Who taught** (programmed the genes and the essential qualities) **by the Pen.** (That is) **Taught man that which he knew not.**" (Quran 96:1-5)

178. "**...And say to those who were given the knowledge of Reality** – *sunnatullah,* **and** [to] **the unlearned** (those who are ignorant of this knowledge; the dualists), '**Have you accepted Islam?**' **And if they submit to this understanding they are on the right path; but if they turn away** – **then upon you is only the** [duty of] **notification...**" (Quran 3:20)

179. "**And you did not recite any scripture** (like the Torah and the Bible) **before** (the KNOWLEDGE we disclosed), **nor did you inscribe one with your right hand** (hence, he may be literate in the general sense[35]). **Otherwise** (had you been reciting and inscribing) **the falsifiers would surely have had doubt.**" (Quran 29:48)

180. "**But this is an honored Quran in a preserved tablet** (*Lawh-i Mahfuz*; the unmanifest knowledge of Allah and *sunnatullah*)." (Quran 85:21-22)

181. "*Ha Miim.* **By the Knowledge that clearly discloses the reality, indeed we have made it an Arabic Quran so that you might** (understand it and) **use your reasoning to evaluate it!**" (Quran 43:1-3)

182. "**...We have not neglected a single thing in the READable** (**Book**) **of the created existence!...**" (Quran 6:38)

183. "**It is HU who has revealed to you the KNOWLEDGE** (Book); **in which there are verses** [that are] **precise** (clear and net to understand) – **they comprise the foundation of the Knowledge** (Book) – **and others that are metaphoric** (symbolic expressions). **As for those in whose hearts there is deviation** [from truth; ill

---

[35] See Quran 25:05

intent], **they will follow the metaphoric verses, interpreting them for the purpose of creating discord. Only Allah knows its [true] interpretation** [i.e. the exact messages these verses denote]. **But those firm in knowledge (deep contemplators) say, 'We believe in it. All [of it] is from our *Rabb*.' And no one can discern this except those who have reached the essence** (the enlightened ones with whom Allah hears, sees and speaks[36])." (Quran 3:7)

184. "And these examples (symbolic language) We present to mankind so they will contemplate." (Quran 59:21)

185. "...And say 'My *Rabb*, increase my knowledge.'" (Quran 20:114)

186. "...To whom We had given (gifted) grace (enabling him to experience his Reality) **and had manifested through him Our Knowledge** (the manifestation of divine attributes as the pleasing self [*nafs-i mardiyya*])." (Quran 18:65)

187. "...Say, 'Can those who know be equal to those who do not know? Only those with deep contemplative intellects can discern this'..." (Quran 39:9)

188. "And your *Rabb* revealed to the bee..." (Quran 16:68)

189. "And there is no animate creature on [or within] the earth or bird that flies with two wings (knowledge and power) except [that they are] communities (formed with an order based on a specific system) **like you!"** (Quran 6:38)

190. "...Indeed, the grace of Allah is near the doers of good (the grace of Allah reaches you by the hand that delivers it)." (Quran 7:56)

191. "...The (tree's) oil (the observation of the reality in consciousness) **would almost glow even if untouched by fire** (active cleansing)... **Light upon light!** (The individualized manifestation of the knowledge of the Names)..." (Quran 24:35)

---

[36] "When the servant approaches Me through his supererogatory acts, I love him, and when I love him I become his ears with which he hears, and I become his eyes with which he sees, and I become his tongue with which he speaks, and I become his hand with which he takes." (Hadith Qudsi)

192. "**Indeed, we offered the Trust** (living conscious of the Names) **to the heavens** (consciousness of the self, ego) **and the earth** (the body) **and the mountains** (the organs), **and they declined to bear it** (their Name compositions did not have the capacity to manifest it) **and feared it; but man** (the consciousness to manifest the Names that compose vicegerency) **undertook to bear it. Indeed, he is unjust** (insufficient in duly living his reality) **and ignorant** (of the knowledge of His infinite Names)." (Quran 33:72)

193. "**And those who strive** (against their egos) **to reach Us, We will surely enable them to reach Our ways** (by enabling them to realize their innermost essential reality... The ability to observe the manifestations of Allah's names ubiquitously). **Indeed Allah is with those who have certainty** (those who turn to Allah as though they see Him, i.e. the manifestations of the qualities of His Names)." (Quran 29:69)

194. "**Except for those who have believed** (in their essential reality) **and applied the requirements of their faith...**" (Quran 103:3)

195. "**...Well-pleased is Allah with them, and well-pleased are they with Him** (the reflections of divine qualities)**...**" (Quran 98:8)

196. "**...And their *Rabb* will give them pure wine** (the euphoric state caused by the exposure to the reality... all these descriptions pertaining to paradise, are similes and figurative representations as mentioned in verses 13:35 and 47:15. This should not be forgotten)" (Quran 76:21)

197. "**The hue of Allah! And what can be better than being colored with the hue of Allah?**" (Quran 2:138)

198. "**And never will Allah fail to fulfill His promise.**" (Quran 3:9)

199. "**As for he who gives** (both *of* himself, i.e. his constructed identity, and *from* himself, i.e. from that which is valuable for him) **and protects himself, and believes** (confirms) **the Most Beautiful** (Names) (to be his essential reality), **We will ease him towards ease. But as for he who withholds and considers himself free of need** (of purification and protection) **and denies the Most Beautiful**

(to be his essential reality), **We will ease him toward the most difficult** (to a life veiled from the knowledge of the Reality and the *sunnatullah*)!" (Quran 92:5-10)

200. "...Pilgrimage to the House (Kaaba, the abode of Allah in one's heart) **is the right of Allah** (the qualities of the Names in one's essence) **upon all people who have the means to undertake it..."** (Quran 3:97)

201. "Fight them; (so that) **Allah will punish them through your hands and will disgrace them..."** (Quran 9:14)

202. "You transform the night into the day, and You transform the day into the night; and You bring the living out of the dead, and You bring the dead out of the living. And You give provision (both limited sustenance for the corporeal life and infinite life sustenance pertaining to the realization of one's inner reality and it's benefits) **to whom You will without account."** (Quran 3:27)

203. "Indeed We have created you, and given you form. Then We said to the angels, 'Prostrate to Adam (in respect of Adam being the manifestation of the totality of Allah's Names)'; **so they all prostrated** (realized their nothingness in the sight of the manifestation of Allah's Names), **except for Iblis**[37]. **He was not of those who prostrated** (He was of the *jinn*; an ego based existence)." (Quran 7:11)

204. "Thereupon Satan whispered suspicions to them (to make them aware of their ego and corporeality)..." (Quran 7:20)

205. "And he swore to them, 'Indeed, I am from among the advisors.'" (Quran 7:21)

206. "Thus he deceived them (by imposing deluding thoughts, making them think they are the physical body; drawing their attention to their corporeality)." (Quran 7:22)

---

[37] Iblis is the name given to a specific *jinn*-based existence the lineage of which continues to serve the same function. The word Satan, on the other hand, is a symbol of reference to a state of existence driven by the ego and corporeality. Those who possess satanic attributes do not believe in an eternal life after the death of the physical body, and reject the knowledge that the Names of Allah comprise their essence.

207. **"And Adam disobeyed his *Rabb*** (succumbed to his ego), **and his way of life erred** (as a result of being veiled to the reality of the Names comprising his essence).**"** (Quran 20:121)

208. **"And Satan** (their ego) **had made pleasing to them their deeds and averted them from the** (righteous) **path... Though they were endowed with the ability to perceive the reality."** (Quran 29:38)

209. **"And** [mention] **when We said to the angels, 'Prostrate to Adam,' and all but Iblis prostrated. He was of the *jinn*...** (thus in favor of his ego) **He disobeyed the command of his *Rabb*** (he did not have the knowledge of reality [the *jinni* have no apprehension of the knowledge of reality], they live purely by the ego. A.H.).**"** (Quran 18:50)

210. **"And recall when your *Rabb* said to the angels, 'Indeed I will create a human being from clay** (water plus minerals).**' So when I have formed him** (by programming his brain) **and breathed**[38] **into him** (became manifest to form the brain) **of My spirit. So the angels prostrated, all of them entirely. Except Iblis; he** (relying on his mind) **was arrogant and became of the deniers of the knowledge of Truth** (those who cannot recognize the essence/reality of others due to their egos).**"** (Quran 38:71-72-73-74)

211. **"**[Allah] **said, 'What prevented you from prostrating when I commanded you?'** [Iblis] **said, 'I am better than him. You created me from fire** (radiation – a specific frequency of wave. Note that the word fire [*naar*] in this verse is the same as the word used in reference to hellfire. This is worth contemplating upon! A.H.) **and created him from clay** (matter).**'** [Allah] **said, 'Descend from your rank, for this rank is not for arrogance and feeling superior over others. Go! Indeed, you have debased yourself.'"** (Quran 7:12-13)

---

[38] The word 'breath' which is '*nafh*' in Arabic literally means to blow out, i.e. to project explicitly, to manifest, to materialize.

212. **"[Iblis] said, 'Reprieve me until the Day they are resurrected** (after death).'" (Quran 7:14)

213. **"[Iblis] said, 'Because You have led me astray,** (*yudhillu man yashau* = based on the reality that He leads astray whom He wills), **I shall most certainly sit on Your straight path** (*sirat al-mustaqim*) **to prevent them. Then I will come to them from before them** (by provoking ambition in them and glorifying their sense of self [ego] to lead them to the denial of the truth) **and from behind them** (by imposing delusive ideas in them and leading them to disguised forms of *shirq* [duality]) **and on their right** (by inspiring them to do 'good deeds' that will take them away from You) **and on their left** (by beautifying misdeeds and making the wrong appear as right)... **And You will find most of them as ungrateful to You** (unable to evaluate what You have given them).'" (Quran 7:16-17)

214. **"[Iblis] said, 'I swear by your might** (the unchallengeable power within my essence denoted by the secret of the letter B), **I will surely mislead them all** (deviate them from spirituality, by making them confine their existence to their physical body and pursuing bodily pleasures). **Except, among them, who are pure in essence** (those to whom You have bestowed the experience of their essential reality).'" (Quran 38:82-83)

215. **"Allah has cursed (Iblis) for he had said, 'I will surely take from among Your servants a significant portion. And I will mislead them, and I will arouse in them** (sinful, bodily, empty) **desires, and I will command them so they slit the ears of cattle** (as sacrifice), **and I will command them so they will alter the creation of Allah.' And whoever takes Satan** (bodily temptations; ego) **as master instead of Allah has certainly suffered a great loss. Satan promises them and arouses false hope and desire in them. But Satan does not promise anything except delusion."** (Quran 4:118-120)

216. **"And certainly, upon you is My curse** (separation from Me; inability to experience your essential reality, being trapped within your ego) **until the Day of Recompense** (the period in which the reality of the system will become clearly evident and thus experienced)." (Quran 38:78)

217. "[Allah] said, 'Descend (to the constricted lower state of bodily existence from a life governed by pure forces) as enemies to one another (the duality of body & consciousness)...'" (Quran 7:24)

218. "You cannot turn (those who are pure in essence) against Him. Except he who is to enter the Hellfire." (Quran 37:162-163)

219. "Verily Iblis proved his assumption (regarding man) to be correct, except for some of the believers they all followed him. And yet he (Iblis/the *jinn*) had no influential power at all over them! We only did this to reveal the distinction between those who truly believe in the eternal life to come and those who are in doubt thereof..." (Quran 34:20-21)

220. "'O communities of *jinn* and mankind, did there not come to you Rasuls from among you, relating to you My messages pointing to reality and warning you of the coming of this Day?' They will say, 'We bear witness against ourselves'; and the worldly life** (they had conjured based on corporeality) **had deluded them, and they will bear witness against themselves that they were deniers of the knowledge of reality." (Quran 6:130)

221. "And the *jinn* We created before from '*samum*' fire** (an infusing microwave radiation that is harmful to the astral body)." (Quran 15:27)

222. "And He created the jann** (the invisible beings, a type of jinn) **from a smokeless flame of fire** (radiation, radiant energy, electromagnetic wave body)." (Quran 55:15)

223. "And [mention, O Muhammad], when We directed to you a group of the *jinn*, so that they may listen to the Quran. And when they were ready for it, they said, 'Be silent!' And when the provision came to place, they went back to their people as warners. They said, 'O our people, indeed we have heard a Knowledge revealed after Moses confirming what was before it which guides to the truth and to a straight path** (*tariq al-mustaqim*; knowledge that leads to the realization of one's servitude to Allah, with or without their consent) **O our people, respond to the DAI'ALLAH** (the *jinn* perceived him as the Dai'Allah not the **Rasulullah**; misused words such as 'messenger' denoting a courier of information derive from this word) **and believe in him; Allah will forgive for you some of your sins**[39] **and protect you from a great suffering...'"** (Quran 46:29-31)

224. "Our inadequate understanding has been making us claim foolish things about Allah! We had thought that mankind and the *jinn* **would never speak a lie about Allah. And yet there were men and women from mankind who sought refuge in men and women from the** *jinn,* **thereby increasing** (provoking each other) **in excessive** (carnal) **behavior."** (Quran 72:4-6)

225. "They turn to lifeless female deities in His stead, and hence they turn to none but stubborn useless Satan (ego)**."** (Quran 4:117)

226. "Indeed, they (those who went astray) **had taken the satans** (the deviators) **as allies instead of Allah, and they consider themselves as rightly guided."** (Quran 7:30)

227. "Yet they attributed the *jinn* (invisible beings) **as partners onto Allah – while He** (Allah) **has created them** (the qualities they manifest are comprised of Allah's names)**..."** (Quran 6:100)

228. "And we have appointed for them companions (those with satanic ideas from amongst the *jinn* and man) **who made attractive to them their actions and desires. And the sentence concerning the** *jinn* **and man that had passed before them has now come into effect upon them. Indeed, they were [all] losers."** (Quran 41:25)

229. "And they have assumed between Him (Allah) **and the** *jinn* (conscious beings outside the human capacity of perception) **a connection** (i.e. associated divinity to them)**, but the** *jinn* **know well that, verily, they** [who made such assumptions] **shall indeed be summoned** (will realize such a connection does not actually exist!)**."** (Quran 37:158)

230. "Indeed, he (Iblis and his lineage of *jinn*) **has no power over those who believe** (that their *Rabb* is sufficient) **and place their trust in their** *Rabb.* **His power is only over those who take**

---

[39] The forgiving of a sin means the elimination of the ego and the awareness that existence is none other than the manifestation of the Names.

him as a guardian (who follow the ideas he imposes upon them) **and those who associate partners with their *Rabb*.**" (Quran 16:99-100)

231. **"The Day when He will gather** (resurrect) **them together** [and say], **'O community of *jinn*, you have truly possessed** (misled from reality) **the vast majority of mankind.' And their allies among mankind will say, 'Our *Rabb*, we mutually benefited from each other, and we have** [now] **reached our term, which you appointed for us.' He will say, 'The Fire is your residence, wherein you will abide eternally, except for what Allah wills...'"** (Quran 6:128)

232. **"Did I not enjoin upon you** (inform you), **O children of Adam, that you not serve Satan** (body/bodily and unconscious state of existence deprived of the knowledge of reality; ego driven existence) [for] **indeed, he** (this state of unconsciousness) **is to you a clear enemy! And that you serve only Me** (experience and feel the requisites of the reality), [as] **this is the straight path** (*sirat al-mustaqim*). **Verily, this unconscious state** (the assumption that you are merely the physical body prone to perish) **has already led astray most of you. Did you not use your reason?"** (Quran 36:60-62)

233. **"He called to his *Rabb*** (the reality of the Names comprising his essence), **'Indeed, Satan** (the feeling of being this body) **has given me hardship and torment.'"** (Quran 38:41)

234. **"And say, 'My *Rabb*** (the protective names within my essence), **I seek refuge in You from the incitements of the satans** (that call to corporeality). **And I seek refuge in You** (the protective names within my essence), **my *Rabb*, lest they be present with me.'"** (Quran 23:97-98)

235. **"O communities of *jinn* and mankind, if you are able to pass beyond the regions of the heavens and the earth, then pass** (live without a body!). **You cannot pass except by power** (the manifestation of Allah's power attribute on you). **So, this being the reality, which of the blessings of your *Rabb*** (the reality of the Names comprising your essence – your consciousness and body) **will you deny? There will be sent upon** (both of) **you a flame of**

fire and smoke (ambiguity and confusion in your consciousness), **and you will not be successful.**" (Quran 55:33-35)

236. "And when (during death) **the heaven** (the identity; the sense of self) **is split asunder and** (the reality) **becomes** (undeniably clear and the ego-self disappears) **burnt oil colored, like a rose**[40] (the reality is observed)! **So, this being the reality, which of the blessings of your *Rabb*** (the reality of the Names comprising your essence – your consciousness and body) **will you deny?**" (Quran 55:37-38)

237. "Then on that Day none among men or *jinn* will be asked about his sin (they will begin to live the natural consequences of their deeds)!" (Quran 55:39)

238. "Certainly you will change dimensions and transform into bodies befitting those dimensions!" (Quran 84:19)

---

[40] In Sufism, rose is the symbol of the observation of reality.

ABOUT THE AUTHOR

Ahmed Hulusi (Born January 21, 1945, Istanbul, Turkey) contemporary Islamic philosopher. From 1965 to this day he has written close to 30 books. His books are written based on Sufi wisdom and explain Islam through scientific principles. His established belief that the knowledge of Allah can only be properly shared without any expectation of return has led him to offer all of his works which include books, articles, and videos free of charge via his web-site. In 1970 he started examining the art of spirit evocation and linked these subjects parallel references in the Quran (smokeless flames and flames instilling pores). He found that these references were in fact pointing to luminous energy which led him to write *Spirit, Man, Jinn* while working as a journalist for the Aksam newspaper in Turkey. Published in 1985, his work called '*Mysteries of Man (Insan ve Sirlari)*' was Hulusi's first foray into decoding the messages of the Quran filled with metaphors and examples through a scientific backdrop. In 1991 he published *A Guide to Prayer and Dhikr (Dua and Zikir)*' where he explains how the repetition of certain prayers and words can lead to the realization of the divine attributes inherent within our essence through increased brain capacity. In 2009 he completed his final work, '*The Key to the Quran through reflections of the Knowledge of Allah*' which encompasses the understanding of leading Sufi scholars such as Abdulkarim al Jili, Abdul-Qadir Gilani, Muhyiddin Ibn al-Arabi, Imam Rabbani, Ahmed ar-Rifai, Imam Ghazali, and Razi, and which approached the messages of the Quran through the secret Key of the letter 'B'.